Instant Effective Caching with Ehcache

Extend the capabilities of your caching layer by integrating Ehcache into your Java Enterprise projects

Daniel Wind

BIRMINGHAM - MUMBAI

Instant Effective Caching with Ehcache

Copyright © 2013 Packt Publishing

All rights reserved. No part of this book may be reproduced, stored in a retrieval system, or transmitted in any form or by any means, without the prior written permission of the publisher, except in the case of brief quotations embedded in critical articles or reviews.

Every effort has been made in the preparation of this book to ensure the accuracy of the information presented. However, the information contained in this book is sold without warranty, either express or implied. Neither the author, nor Packt Publishing, and its dealers and distributors will be held liable for any damages caused or alleged to be caused directly or indirectly by this book.

Packt Publishing has endeavored to provide trademark information about all of the companies and products mentioned in this book by the appropriate use of capitals. However, Packt Publishing cannot guarantee the accuracy of this information.

First published: August 2013

Production Reference: 1240813

Published by Packt Publishing Ltd.
Livery Place
35 Livery Street
Birmingham B3 2PB, UK.

ISBN 978-1-78216-038-0

www.packtpub.com

Credits

Author
Daniel Wind

Reviewers
Dylan Stamat
Mikael Sundberg

Acquisition Editors
Kartikey Pandey
Antony Lowe

Commissioning Editor
Shreerang Deshpande

Technical Editor
Amit Ramadas

Project Coordinator
Esha Thakker

Proofreader
Linda Morris

Graphics
Abhinash Sahu

Production Coordinator
Zahid Shaikh

Cover Work
Zahid Shaikh

Cover Image
Nilesh R. Mohite

About the Author

Daniel Wind is a Software Architect from Costa Rica who is passionate about coding and implementing scientific paradigms to achieve innovative solutions. He has worked for companies helping them by providing architecture consultancy as well as software engineering, especially in the mobile space.

Daniel started as a physics geek who got into computer science at the very moment he saw his first C-based simulation program in action. He fell in love with it and became addicted. He then moved to business-oriented software where he applied actuarial mathematics and software engineering to provide data forecast models, neural networks, and system statistics. He is an advocate of the Java technology as the industry's "new Cobol", in the sense that Java Enterprise and the de-facto solutions available solve almost all business problems.

Daniel's spare time interests range from business software needs to 3D mobile games. The latter one is an interesting topic he's up to by using the Android SDK and Blackberry NDK. When he's not coding or writing, he loves traveling with his family, listening to Coldplay, or watching his longtime hero Bear Grylls.

Acknowledgments

This book is dedicated to my daughters María Paula and María Celeste for being such a beautiful gift from life. I love you.

Writing a book is a time-consuming, but enjoyable, experience that lets you view life and people on a different perspective. You specially notice how people around help you even if not directly related to your work.

I would like to first thank God for blessing me and my family everyday. I thank my parents for giving me the tools needed for success. I thank my wife, who has been incredibly patient and supportive even when I cancelled hangouts at the last minute for some writing. I would also like to thank my brother Manfred who helped me with suggestions and support. Many thanks to my IT colleagues who read the draft and pointed me to improvements.

Last, but not least, I really thank Esha Takker, Priyanka Shah, and Poonam Jain from Packt Publishing for being so patient during the book writing process. And, of course, Ehcache adopters worldwide and Terracotta folks; without you Ehcache would not be what it is.

About the Reviewers

Dylan Stamat is a long time technologist and founder at VerticalChange. With roots in Business Intelligence, he moved into software development and helped bootstrap a number of successful startups. Dylan went on to grow a software consulting firm as CTO, and helped draft technical strategies for a variety of Fortune 500 companies, including ESPN, Cisco, and Google. He now spends his time helping the social sector help others with the help of VerticalChange.

Mikael Sundberg is a Swedish developer with a passion for learning new things and keeping it simple. He tries to find the right tool for the job and keeping the code clean. He has worked as a PHP and Java developer for several years and is currently a Ruby developer.

www.PacktPub.com

Support files, eBooks, discount offers and more

You might want to visit www.PacktPub.com for support files and downloads related to your book.

Did you know that Packt offers eBook versions of every book published, with PDF and ePub files available? You can upgrade to the eBook version at www.PacktPub.com and as a print book customer, you are entitled to a discount on the eBook copy. Get in touch with us at service@packtpub.com for more details.

At www.PacktPub.com, you can also read a collection of free technical articles, sign up for a range of free newsletters and receive exclusive discounts and offers on Packt books and eBooks.

http://PacktLib.PacktPub.com

Do you need instant solutions to your IT questions? PacktLib is Packt's online digital book library. Here, you can access, read and search across Packt's entire library of books.

Why Subscribe?

- Fully searchable across every book published by Packt
- Copy and paste, print and bookmark content
- On demand and accessible via web browser

Free Access for Packt account holders

If you have an account with Packt at www.PacktPub.com, you can use this to access PacktLib today and view nine entirely free books. Simply use your login credentials for immediate access.

Table of Contents

Preface	**1**
Instant Effective Caching with Ehcache	**7**
Configuration patterns (Simple)	7
Handling events and exceptions (Intermediate)	12
Spring Cache Abstraction (Intermediate)	17
Caching web fragments (Intermediate)	22
Hibernate second-level caching (Intermediate)	26
The Ehcache Search API (Advanced)	30
The custom eviction algorithm (Advanced)	36
Out-of-process distributed caching (Intermediate)	41
Ehcache monitoring and logging (Intermediate)	47
Ehcache transactional support (Advanced)	51
Ehcache and Terracotta Server Array (Advanced)	57
Datasource read overloading (Intermediate)	63
Appendix A: Core Concepts	**67**
Cache usage patterns	69

Preface

Caching is the de-facto mechanism to make systems faster and improve the overall performance. If you are a Java developer looking for an easy-to-integrate library that provides all benefits from caching to even more, this book is for you. Ehcache, from Terracota, is among the best of the caching engine solutions for Java projects.

Instant Effective Caching with Ehcache is a comprehensive recipe-styled guide for integrating the Ehcache library into your Java projects. Its purpose is to provide a hands-on approach from the beginning by showing common scenarios that developers face when starting to contemplate Ehcache as their cache engine. Running examples are included to illustrate every recipe's concepts as well as to provide easy-to-setup templates that you can re-use for your own projects.

You will get the know-how on configuring and using Ehcache effectively. We will explore various situations you can encounter in production environments; so this guide is useful not only for those who are just learning the technology, but also for those who want to implement advanced techniques in their daily jobs with Ehcache.

What this book covers

Configuration patterns (Simple) introduces the Ehcache library configuration patterns, namely declarative or programmatic. You'll learn how to configure Ehcache in both ways and will have a template project structure that you can tweak for other projects.

Handling events and exceptions (Intermediate) explains how to react against Ehcache events and exceptions. You will learn how to declaratively configure caching for this purpose and set up a cache proxy for advanced configuration.

Spring Cache Abstraction (Intermediate) explores the Spring Cache Abstraction feature and also explains how Ehcache is easily integrated. You will also learn the configuration needed to achieve caching effectively.

Caching web fragments (Intermediate) helps you learn what fragment caching is and how to implement it in any Java servlet-based framework. We will revise the configuration structure and the filter flow so that they can be re-used on any project.

Hibernate second-level caching (Intermediate) explains the concepts and details about configuration as well as a simple implementation of Ehcache-Hibernate integration in Java projects for reference.

The Ehcache Search API (Advanced) helps you implement a custom search for cached objects based on their properties rather than keys. You will learn to adapt the Ehcache search engine to your project OOP model.

The custom eviction algorithm (Advanced) helps you dive into the eviction world and discover how to tell Ehcache engine to evict objects according to an algorithm we want to implement from scratch.

Out-of-process distributed caching (Intermediate) shows you how to implement distributed caching using the Ehcache server RESTful module. We will explore the details and concepts of out-of-process caching.

Ehcache monitoring and logging (Intermediate) helps you learn how to set up a simple caching monitoring system using open source software. We will also examine how to integrate the Ehcache default SLF4j logging with Log4j.

Ehcache transactional support (Advanced) shows you how to integrate Ehcache in a transactional operation. We will examine Ehcache's new local transaction capabilities to rollback operations if something goes wrong.

Ehcache and Terracotta Server Array (Advanced) helps you delve into the clustered environments and also explains how they affect caching. We will focus on TSA and its seamless support for Ehcache.

Datasource read overloading (Intermediate) helps you investigate what a thundering herd problem is and how Ehcache can help us to solve this sort of problem relatively easily.

Appendix A, Core Concepts dives into the theoretical concepts behind caching theory and synthesizes the most important aspects of this technology that every professional developer needs to be aware of.

Appendix B, Setting Up the Source Code shows you how to build and run the demo source code by providing concise visual aided instructions to help you get up and running in no time. You can download this appendix from `http://www.packtpub.com/sites/default/files/downloads/03800S_Appendix_B_Setting_Up_the_Source_Code.pdf`.

What you need for this book

For a successful understanding of the concepts exposed in this book, you will need the following software:

- Java 6 or later
- Maven 3 or later
- Eclipse (optional)

Ehcache and other dependencies will be specified when needed.

Who this book is for

This book is for Java developers who want to implement caching in their Java projects. Intermediate Java programming skills are required.

Conventions

In this book, you will find a number of styles of text that distinguish between different kinds of information. Here are some examples of these styles, and an explanation of their meaning.

Code words in text are shown as follows: "Add a cache configuration to your `ehcache.xml` file."

A block of code is set as follows:

```xml
<dependency>
  <groupId>net.sf.ehcache</groupId>
  <artifactId>ehcache</artifactId>
  <version>2.6.0</version>
  <type>pom</type>
</dependency>
<dependency>
  <groupId>org.slf4j</groupId>
  <artifactId>slf4j-log4j12</artifactId>
  <version>1.7.2</version>
</dependency>
```

When we wish to draw your attention to a particular part of a code block, the relevant lines or items are set in bold:

```
//register our custom event listener
cache.getCacheEventNotificationService().registerListener(newCustomEventListener());
```

> Warnings or important notes appear in a box like this.

> Tips and tricks appear like this.

Reader feedback

Feedback from our readers is always welcome. Let us know what you think about this book—what you liked or may have disliked. Reader feedback is important for us to develop titles that you really get the most out of.

To send us general feedback, simply send an e-mail to feedback@packtpub.com, and mention the book title via the subject of your message.

If there is a book that you need and would like to see us publish, please send us a note in the **SUGGEST A TITLE** form on www.packtpub.com or e-mail suggest@packtpub.com.

If there is a topic that you have expertise in and you are interested in either writing or contributing to a book, see our author guide on www.packtpub.com/authors.

Customer support

Now that you are the proud owner of a Packt book, we have a number of things to help you to get the most from your purchase.

Downloading the example code

You can download the example code files for all Packt books you have purchased from your account at http://www.PacktPub.com. If you purchased this book elsewhere, you can visit http://www.PacktPub.com/support and register to have the files e-mailed directly to you.

Errata

Although we have taken every care to ensure the accuracy of our content, mistakes do happen. If you find a mistake in one of our books—maybe a mistake in the text or the code—we would be grateful if you would report this to us. By doing so, you can save other readers from frustration and help us improve subsequent versions of this book. If you find any errata, please report them by visiting http://www.packtpub.com/support, selecting your book, clicking on the **errata submission form** link, and entering the details of your errata. Once your errata are verified, your submission will be accepted and the errata will be uploaded on our website, or added to any list of existing errata, under the Errata section of that title. Any existing errata can be viewed by selecting your title from http://www.packtpub.com/support.

Piracy

Piracy of copyright material on the Internet is an ongoing problem across all media. At Packt, we take the protection of our copyright and licenses very seriously. If you come across any illegal copies of our works, in any form, on the Internet, please provide us with the location address or website name immediately so that we can pursue a remedy.

Please contact us at copyright@packtpub.com with a link to the suspected pirated material.

We appreciate your help in protecting our authors, and our ability to bring you valuable content.

Questions

You can contact us at questions@packtpub.com if you are having a problem with any aspect of the book, and we will do our best to address it.

Instant Effective Caching with Ehcache

Caching is the de-facto mechanism to make systems faster and improve the overall performance. If you are a Java developer looking for an easy-to-integrate library that provides all the benefits from caching and even more, this book is for you. Ehcache, from Terracota, is among the best caching engine solutions for Java projects.

Instant Effective Caching with Ehcache is a comprehensive recipe-styled guide for integrating Ehcache library into your Java projects. Its purpose is to provide a hands-on approach from the beginning by showing common scenarios that developers face while starting to contemplate Ehcache as their cache engine. Running examples are included to illustrate every recipe's concepts as well as to provide easy-to-setup templates that you can re-use for your own projects.

You will get the know-how on configuring and using Ehcache effectively. We will explore the various situations you can encounter in production environments; so this guide is useful not only for those who are just learning the technology, but also for those who want to implement advanced techniques in their daily job with Ehcache.

Configuration patterns (Simple)

In this recipe, we will cover the following topics:

- Getting the Ehcache library
- Integrating Ehcache into a Maven project
- Declarative configuration through XML
- Programmatic configuration – CacheManager and CacheConfiguration

Getting ready

Ehcache can be configured in two simple ways: either declarative or programmatic. The question is what to configure. Let's think about what we would need to configure:

- We need some sort of name or ID in order to refer to the cache component
- How many elements do we want to store in the memory?
- Do we want to store those elements in the cache forever?
- If the answer for the preceding query is *No*, how long do we want elements to live?
- Do we want to store to disk as well?
- If the answer for the preceding query is *Yes*, how many elements do we want to store on disk?

As you will see, this is practically all you need to configure Ehcache. An important note here is that some of these properties are dynamically configurable (you can change their values at runtime). At a glance, you can dynamically change the elements' lifespan, as well as the number of elements you can store (memory and/or disk).

Refer to the `recipe1` project directory within the source code bundle for a fully working sample of this recipe content and for further information related to this topic.

How to do it...

1. Add Ehcache and SLF4J dependencies to your `POM.xml` file.

   ```xml
   <dependency>
     <groupId>net.sf.ehcache</groupId>
     <artifactId>ehcache</artifactId>
     <version>2.6.0</version>
     <type>pom</type>
   </dependency>
   <dependency>
     <groupId>org.slf4j</groupId>
     <artifactId>slf4j-log4j12</artifactId>
     <version>1.7.2</version>
   </dependency>
   ```

2. Create a blank XML file called `ehcache.xml` in the `resources` directory with the following content:

   ```xml
   <?xml version="1.0" encoding="UTF-8"?>
   <ehcache xmlns:xsi="http://www.w3.org/2001/XMLSchema-instance"
   ```

```xml
            xsi:noNamespaceSchemaLocation="ehcache.xsd"
            updateCheck="false" monitoring="off"
dynamicConfig="false">

            <!-- Uncomment if diskStore is desired -->
            <!--<diskStore path="java.io.tmpdir"/> -->

            <!-- Default Cache configuration (super configuration)
-->

            <defaultCache maxEntriesLocalHeap="0"
                          eternal="false"
                    timeToIdleSeconds="1200"
                    timeToLiveSeconds="1200"/>

            <!-- Sample Cache :: This cache has a maximum of 100
    elements in memory.
            There is no overflow to disk, so 100 is also the maximum
    cache size.
            -->
            <cache name="objectCache"
              maxEntriesLocalHeap="100"
              eternal="true"/>

</ehcache>
```

3. Load the configuration file and set the `Cache` objects.

   ```
   import net.sf.ehcache.CacheManager;
   import net.sf.ehcache.Ehcache;

   private static final String EHCACHE_CONFIG = "src/main/resources/ehcache.xml";
   private static final string CACHE_NAME = "objectCache";

   CacheManager manager = new CacheManager(EHCACHE_CONFIG);
   Ehcache cache = manager.getCache(CACHE_NAME);

   //do operations with cache reference
   ```

4. Load the configuration programmatically. In this case, there is no need to create an XML file. This is an optional step.

   ```
   import net.sf.ehcache.CacheManager;
   import net.sf.ehcache.Ehcache;

   Configuration cacheManagerConfiguration = new Configuration();
   ```

Instant Effective Caching with Ehcache

```
            CacheConfiguration cacheConfiguration = new CacheConfiguration("ob
jectCache", 100)
                            .eternal(true)
                            .maxEntriesLocalHeap(100);

            cacheManagerConfiguration.addCache(cacheConfiguration);

            CacheManager manager = new CacheManager(cacheManagerConfigurati
on);

            Ehcache cache = manager.getEhcache("objectCache");

            //do operations with cache reference
```

How it works...

Configuring Ehcache is a very straightforward task. We start by creating a configuration file, `ehcache.xml`, to perform Ehcache configuration.

```
    ...
            <!-- Sample Cache => This cache has a maximum of 100 elements
    in memory.
                There is no overflow to disk, so 100 is also the maximum
    cache size.
            -->
            <cache name="objectCache"
                maxEntriesLocalHeap="100"
                eternal="true"/>
    ...
```

Once you have declared your configuration parameters, create an instance of the Ehcache's library, `CacheManager`, specifying the location of the file.

```
    ...
    CacheManager manager = new CacheManager(EHCACHE_CONFIG);
    ...
```

Finally, create an instance of the Ehcache object by referencing the `CacheManager` instance.

```
    ...
    Ehcache cache = manager.getCache(CACHE_NAME);
    ...
```

There's more...

An XML-based configuration is quite common in Java projects. However, you may encounter situations where this is not possible; so you require some more flexibility. Ehcache can also be conveniently configured programmatically in a very simplistic manner.

Create a `Configuration` class instance to hold our configuration for the `CacheManager` instance.

```
Configuration configurationHolder = new Configuration();
```

Create a `CacheConfiguration` class instance to define our caching properties.

```
CacheConfiguration cacheConfiguration =
    new CacheConfiguration("cacheName", 100)
                        .eternal(true)
                        .maxEntriesLocalHeap(100);
CacheConfiguration cacheConfiguration = new
CacheConfiguration("cacheName", 100)
                        .eternal(true)
                    .maxEntriesLocalHeap(100);
```

Add `CacheConfiguration` to `configurationHolder`:

```
configurationHolder.addCache(cacheConfiguration);
```

Create `CacheManager` with the new configuration.

```
CacheManager manager = new CacheManager(configurationHolder);
```

Create a `cache` instance.

```
Ehcache cache = manager.getEhcache("cacheName");
```

> For further reference, you can see a full example of the `ehcache.xml` file with all entries as defined by Terracotta folks here: http://ehcache.org/ehcache.xml.

In this recipe's source code sample you can find a simple Java program targeting Ehcache configuration implementation (declaratively and programmatically). Please refer to *Appendix B, Setting Up the Source Code* (available for download at http://www.packtpub.com/sites/default/files/downloads/0380OS_Appendix_B_Setting_Up_the_Source_Code.pdf) for further information on how to build the recipe demo code.

> **Downloading the example code**
>
> You can download the example code files for all Packt books you have purchased from your account at http://www.packtpub.com. If you purchased this book elsewhere, you can visit http://www.packtpub.com/support and register to have the files e-mailed directly to you.

Instant Effective Caching with Ehcache

Handling events and exceptions (Intermediate)

In this recipe, we will cover the following topics:

- Reacting to the Ehcache Events model
- Ehcache exception custom handling
- Programmatic configuration through a proxy cache reference

In this recipe we show how Ehcache events and exceptions can be intercepted and contributed to our application behavior when errors/things happen. We will demonstrate current ways to configure caching for event handling purposes as well as advanced proxy cache configurations.

Getting ready

Ehcache events and exception handling can be configured in two ways: either declarative or programmatic. Depending on which one you choose you will need to add more code (declarative). In simple words, for overriding the Ehcache default event and exception behavior, you need to add custom implementation for each behavior's interface, namely `CacheEventListener` and `CacheExceptionHandler` (both pertaining to the Ehcache-core API).

If you decide to go the declarative route, you need to be aware that you will also need to create custom `Factory` classes (`CacheEventListenerFactory` and `CacheExceptionHandlerFactory`) and utilize `ClassLoaderUtil` provided by the Ehcache team in order to load these classes.

> Refer to the `recipe2` project directory within the source code bundle for a fully working sample of this recipe content and further information related to this topic.

How to do it...

1. Add Ehcache and SLF4J dependencies to your `POM.xml` file.

    ```
    <dependency>
      <groupId>net.sf.ehcache</groupId>
      <artifactId>ehcache</artifactId>
      <version>2.6.0</version>
      <type>pom</type>
    </dependency>
    <dependency>
    ```

```xml
        <groupId>org.slf4j</groupId>
        <artifactId>slf4j-log4j12</artifactId>
        <version>1.7.2</version>
</dependency>
```

2. Add a cache configuration to your `ehcache.xml` file with the following content:

```xml
<?xml version="1.0" encoding="UTF-8"?>
<ehcache xmlns:xsi="http://www.w3.org/2001/XMLSchema-instance"
         xsi:noNamespaceSchemaLocation="ehcache.xsd"
         updateCheck="false" monitoring="off" dynamicConfig="true">


        <!-- Sample Cache :: This cache has a maximum of 100 elements in memory.
        There is no overflow to disk, so 100 is also the maximum cache size.
        -->
        <cache name="objectCache"
          maxEntriesLocalHeap="100"
          eternal="true"
          memoryStoreEvictionPolicy="FIFO">

        </cache>
</ehcache>
```

3. Load the configuration file and set the Cache Objects and Listeners (programmatically):

```java
import net.sf.ehcache.CacheException;
import net.sf.ehcache.CacheManager;
import net.sf.ehcache.Ehcache;
import net.sf.ehcache.Element;
import net.sf.ehcache.exceptionhandler.ExceptionHandlingDynamicCacheProxy;

private static final String EHCACHE_CONFIG = "src/main/resources/ehcache.xml";
private static final string CACHE_NAME = "objectCache";

CacheManager manager = new CacheManager(EHCACHE_CONFIG);
Ehcache cache = manager.getCache(CACHE_NAME);

//register our custom event listener
cache.getCacheEventNotificationService().registerListener(newCustomEventListener());
```

```
//set our custom exception handler
cache.setCacheExceptionHandler(new CustomExceptionHandler());

//create cache proxy
Ehcache proxiedCache = ExceptionHandlingDynamicCacheProxy.
createProxy(cache);

//replace default with decorated cache
manager.replaceCacheWithDecoratedCache(cache, proxiedCache);
```

4. Create your custom `CacheEventListener`.

   ```
   import net.sf.ehcache.event.CacheEventListener;
   import org.apache.log4j.Logger;

   public class CustomEventListener implements CacheEventListener {

   //implement methods below...
   ```

5. Create your custom `CacheExceptionHandler`.

   ```
   import net.sf.ehcache.exceptionhandler.CacheExceptionHandler;
   import org.apache.log4j.Logger;

   public class CustomExceptionHandler implements
   CacheExceptionHandler {

   //implement methods below...
   ```

That's all you need to do in order to start listening to Ehcache events and handling exceptions.

How it works...

Ehcache dispatches events that we can listen to by appropriately configuring the `cache` instance. From a code perspective, this configuration is a trivial task of registering listeners (and decorating the cache with a proxy if you wish to add exceptions handling). The way you add this configuration is your preference: either declarative or programmatic. We will discuss the programmatic approach first.

We start by adding our cache configuration to our `ehcache.xml` file.

```xml
<cache name="objectCache"
  maxEntriesLocalHeap="100"
  eternal="false"
  memoryStoreEvictionPolicy="FIFO">
```

We then move to configure our `CacheManager` and `cache` instances to tell Ehcache that we want to get notified of events (such as elements being added/removed/updated/expired/evicted from cache) and be aware of cache exceptions. The first thing to do is to register our custom event listener implementation (which we will need to code in a later step).

```
//register our custom event listener
cache.getCacheEventNotificationService().registerListener(new
CustomEventListener());
```

Now let's set our custom exception handler (we will need to code it in a later step).

```
//set our custom exception handler
cache.setCacheExceptionHandler(new CustomExceptionHandler());
```

Once that is done, we need to create a proxy cache that would let us communicate with the Ehcache event dispatcher in order to proxy events and exceptions.

```
//create cache proxy
Ehcache proxiedCache = ExceptionHandlingDynamicCacheProxy.
createProxy(cache);
```

The final step (configuration-related) is to decorate our cache manager with our proxy cache:

```
//replace default with decorated cache
manager.replaceCacheWithDecoratedCache(cache, proxiedCache);
```

By now, we just need to create our custom listener and exception handler. For doing this, we rely on the Ehcache API library that offers two interfaces that we can implement.

```
import net.sf.ehcache.exceptionhandler.CacheExceptionHandler;
...

public class CustomExceptionHandler implements CacheExceptionHandler {

  @Override
  public void onException(Ehcache ehcache, Object key, Exception
exception) {
     log.error("Exception occured in cache instance: " + ehcache.
getName());
  }
}
```

And, the custom event listener is defined as:

```
import net.sf.ehcache.event.CacheEventListener;

public class CacheDelegateEventListener implements CacheEventListener
{
```

Instant Effective Caching with Ehcache

```
    ...

    @Override
    public void notifyElementRemoved(Ehcache cache, Element element)
        throws CacheException {
            log.debug("do something");
    }

    //implement other methods here
    ...
}
```

Now, if you want to use the declarative approach, start by editing your `ehcache.xml` file to add the following entries as children nodes of the defined cache.

```
<cache ...>
...

<!-- Add Cache Event Listener Factory -->
<cacheEventListenerFactory
        class="com.foo.factory.CustomEventListenerFactory"
        properties="logLevel=FINE"
        listenFor="all"/>


<!-- Add Cache Exception Handler Factory -->
<cacheExceptionHandlerFactory
        class="com.foo.factory.CustomExceptionHandlerFactory"
        properties="logLevel=FINE"/>

</cache>
    ...
```

Create the custom event listener factory and the custom exception handler factory in your code by extending the convenient Ehcache factory classes.

```
import net.sf.ehcache.event.CacheEventListener;
import net.sf.ehcache.event.CacheEventListenerFactory;

public class CustomEventListenerFactory extends
    CacheEventListenerFactory {

  @Override
  public CacheEventListener createCacheEventListener(Properties
properties) {
      return CustomEventListener.INSTANCE;
  }

}
```

And, the exception handler factory class is defined as:

```
import net.sf.ehcache.exceptionhandler.CacheExceptionHandler;
import net.sf.ehcache.exceptionhandler.CacheExceptionHandlerFactory;

public class CustomExceptionHandlerFactory extends
   CacheExceptionHandlerFactory {

  @Override
  public CacheExceptionHandler createExceptionHandler(Properties
properties) {
     return CustomExceptionHandler.INSTANCE;
  }
}
```

We still need to create the implementation for `CustomEventListener` and `CustomExceptionHandler` as we did previously. And that is all you need, since the configuration is being handled entirely by Ehcache through the XML entries.

> If your project lives in a cluster (especially Terracotta), you can detect event-related cache on all nodes and get details on node activity. For further information refer to the documentation at `http://www.ehcache.org/documentation/2.4/terracotta/distributed-caching-with-terracotta`.

There's more...

In this recipe's source code sample you can find a full implementation for events management as well as exception handling. It shows a simple program that caches entries from a JSON file and logs according to the event generated. It also reacts to caching exceptions. Please refer to *Appendix B, Setting Up the Source Code* (available for download at `http://www.packtpub.com/sites/default/files/downloads/0380OS_Appendix_B_Setting_Up_the_Source_Code.pdf`) for further information on how to build the recipe demo code.

Spring Cache Abstraction (Intermediate)

In this recipe, we will cover the following topics:

- Including Ehcache in a Spring-based project
- Declarative configuration through XML
- Spring cache abstraction API details

We will examine how to configure Ehcache in Spring-based projects using the Cache Abstraction utility. This allows us to seamlessly integrate both technologies and give our projects enough flexibility to set up the cache in a nonintrusive way.

Getting ready

Ehcache can be easily integrated with the latest Spring Framework. Configuring it is a simple application context configuration and some custom annotated code for handling the cache requirements.

> Refer to the `recipe3` project directory within the source code bundle for a fully working sample of this recipe content and further information related to this topic.

How to do it...

1. Add Ehcache and Spring 3.x Cache Abstraction API dependencies to your `POM.xml` file.

    ```xml
    <dependency>
            <groupId>org.slf4j</groupId>
            <artifactId>slf4j-log4j12</artifactId>
            <version>1.7.2</version>
        </dependency>

        <dependency>
            <groupId>net.sf.ehcache</groupId>
            <artifactId>ehcache-core</artifactId>
          <version>2.6.0</version>
        </dependency>

        <!-- Spring 3 dependencies -->
        <dependency>
          <groupId>org.springframework</groupId>
          <artifactId>spring-core</artifactId>
          <version>3.1.1.RELEASE</version>
        </dependency>

            <dependency>
                <groupId>org.springframework</groupId>
                <artifactId>spring-context-support</artifactId>
                <version>3.1.1.RELEASE</version>
            </dependency>
    ```

2. Create a blank XML file called `ehcache.xml` in the `resources` directory with the following content:

```xml
<?xml version="1.0" encoding="UTF-8"?>
<ehcache xmlns:xsi="http://www.w3.org/2001/XMLSchema-instance"
         xsi:noNamespaceSchemaLocation="ehcache.xsd"
         updateCheck="false"
         monitoring="off"
         dynamicConfig="true">

  <cache name="someCache"
    maxElementsInMemory="50"
    eternal="false"
    overflowToDisk="false"
    memoryStoreEvictionPolicy="LFU"/>

</ehcache>
```

3. Edit your Spring configuration file to include the cache abstraction configuration:

```xml
<?xml version="1.0" encoding="UTF-8"?>
<beans xmlns="http://www.springframework.org/schema/beans"
...
xmlns:cache="http://www.springframework.org/schema/cache"
...
http://www.springframework.org/schema/cache
           http://www.springframework.org/schema/cache/spring-cache.xsd">

    <context:component-scan base-package="com.foo"/>

    <cache:annotation-driven />

    <!-- EhCache Cache Manager Bean -->
    <bean id="cacheManager" name="cacheManager"
          class="org.springframework.cache.ehcache.EhCacheCacheManager"
          p:cache-manager-ref="ehcache"/>


    <!-- EhCache Factory Bean -->
    <bean id="ehcache" name="ehcache"
          class="org.springframework.cache.ehcache.EhCacheManagerFactoryBean"
          p:config-location="classpath:ehcache.xml"
          p:shared="true"/>

        ...
</beans>
```

4. Edit your service/dao objects as follows (DAO recommended):

   ```
   @Cacheable(cacheName="datacache", key="#sampleId",
   condition="sampleId > 100")
   public SampleData getSampleData(String sampleId){
   SampleData data = new SampleData();
   data.setId(sampleId);
   ```

5. Select a method to provide cache eviction and mark it:

   ```
   @CacheEvict(value="sampleData" , allEntries="true")
   public void resetSampleData() {
     //do something
   }
   ```

How it works...

Integrating Ehcache into Spring projects is a quite straightforward process using Spring cache abstraction.

We first create the typical Ehcache configuration (declarative XML or programmatic) with all the required parameters. Then, we edit the Spring application context definition (or Dispatcher Servlet definition in Spring MVC) to add references to the Spring cache schema location:

```
http://www.springframework.org/schema/cache
http://www.springframework.org/schema/cache/spring-cache.xsd">
```

After importing the Spring cache abstraction definition, we need to add support for annotation-driven cache.

```
<cache:annotation-driven  />
```

We now need to specify who the cache manager is as well as the cache factory bean.

```
        <!-- EhCache Cache Manager Bean -->
        <bean id="cacheManager" name="cacheManager"
             class="org.springframework.cache.ehcache.
EhCacheCacheManager"
             p:cache-manager-ref="ehcache"/>


        <!-- EhCache Factory Bean -->
        <bean id="ehcache" name="ehcache"
```

```
         class="org.springframework.cache.ehcache.
EhCacheManagerFactoryBean"
         p:config-location="classpath:ehcache.xml"
         p:shared="true"/>
```

Then, we annotate the DAO implementation to cache data:

```
@Cacheable(cacheName="datacache", key="#sampleId", condition="sampleId
> 100")
public SampleData getSampleData(String sampleId){
...
```

The `Cacheable` annotation simply indicates that the method should be cached once it is populated for the first time (or more accurately, every time the cache layer gets cleaned). It possesses various useful attributes, namely:

- `cacheName`: It must match the cache name in `ehcache.xml` and define the caching conditions for that element (you can also use the `SpEL` value attribute, refer to condition in this list).
- `key`: It represents the cache key whose value is cached. This value should match the argument name in the method that is being set to cacheable. If not declared, the Spring Framework will use a default key generator (unless you specify a custom key generator).
- `condition` (the `SpEL` attribute): It presents a conditional statement to determine whether the element(s) should be cached or not.

Finally, if we want to have a method to perform cache eviction, we proceed as follows:

```
@CacheEvict(value="sampleData" , allEntries="true")
public void resetSampleData() {
  //do something
}
```

This will evict the cached elements within the active cache region. The annotation `@CacheEvict` is useful to mark methods that perform cache eviction (ejecting data from the cache layer). The `allEntries` attribute defines whether you want all cache entries to be cleared or it should be done atomically (per key).

> For more information on Spring Cache Abstraction API standard documentation visit http://static.springsource.org/spring/docs/3.1.0.M1/spring-framework-reference/html/cache.html.

There's more...

In this recipe's source code sample you can find a simple Spring MVC implementation for cache abstraction using Ehcache as the cache provider. It implements the recipe steps and provides insight in greater detail on how to manage configuration dependencies. Please refer to *Appendix B, Setting Up the Source Code* (available for download at http://www.packtpub.com/sites/default/files/downloads/0380OS_Appendix_B_Setting_Up_the_Source_Code.pdf) for further information on how to build the recipe demo code.

Caching web fragments (Intermediate)

In this recipe, we will cover the following topics:

- What Fragment Caching is and its benefits for web projects
- Integrating Fragment Caching using Ehcache and Servlet API

We will examine how to implement fragment caching by integrating Ehcache and the Servlet API. We will cache the header of a web page in order to demonstrate how caching can be achieved for sections of a web page or a full web page if needed.

Getting ready

Fragment Caching is a technique used to cache sections of your web page in order to provide speed and increase performance. It is useful when certain elements of the page change frequently or depend on a complicated state, while other parts do not change so often. The Ehcache library provides a web module with general purpose filters that you can easily integrate in your Java web project.

> Refer to the `recipe4` project directory within the source code bundle for a fully working sample of this recipe content and further information related to this topic.

How to do it...

1. Add Ehcache and Ehcache web module dependencies to your `POM.xml` file.

   ```
   <!-- EhCache WEB Component (required) -->
   <dependency>
     <groupId>net.sf.ehcache</groupId>
     <artifactId>ehcache-web</artifactId>
     <version>2.0.4</version>
   </dependency>
   <dependency>
   ```

```xml
<groupId>net.sf.ehcache</groupId>
<artifactId>ehcache</artifactId>
<version>2.6.0</version>
<type>pom</type>
</dependency>
```

2. Create a blank XML file called ehcache.xml in the resources directory with the following content:

```xml
<?xml version="1.0" encoding="UTF-8"?>
<ehcache xmlns:xsi="http://www.w3.org/2001/XMLSchema-instance"
         xsi:noNamespaceSchemaLocation="ehcache.xsd"
         updateCheck="false"
         monitoring="off"
         dynamicConfig="true">

    <cache name="FullPageCachingFilter"
           maxEntriesLocalHeap="1000"
           eternal="false"
           timeToIdleSeconds="300"
           timeToLiveSeconds="600">
        <persistence strategy="localTempSwap"/>
    </cache>

    <cache name="CustomFragmentCachingFilter"
      maxEntriesLocalHeap="1000"
           eternal="false"
               timeToIdleSeconds="300"
           timeToLiveSeconds="600">
        <persistence strategy="localTempSwap"/>
    </cache>

</ehcache>
```

3. Create and configure a filter in your web.xml file:

```xml
<web-app xmlns="http://java.sun.com/xml/ns/javaee"
xmlns:xsi="http://www.w3.org/2001/XMLSchema-instance"
xsi:schemaLocation="http://java.sun.com/xml/ns/javaee
version="2.5">

...

<!-- EhCache Full Page Cache Filter -->
  <filter>
    <filter-name>FullPageCachingFilter</filter-name>
```

```xml
        <filter-class>
             com.foo.filters.FullPageCachingFilter
        </filter-class>
 </filter>

 <filter-mapping>
   <filter-name>FullPageCachingFilter</filter-name>
   <url-pattern>/application/pageCache.action</url-pattern>
 </filter-mapping>

 <!-- EhCache Fragment Cache Filter -->
 <filter>
   <filter-name>CustomPageFragmentCachingFilter</filter-name>
   <filter-class>
      com.foo.filters.CustomPageFragmentCachingFilter
  </filter-class>
 </filter>

 <filter-mapping>
    <filter-name>CustomPageFragmentCachingFilter</filter-name>
    <url-pattern>/application/fragmentCache.action</url-pattern>
 </filter-mapping>

 ...
```

4. Create your own Servlet filter or specialize the Ehcache filters provided in the web module.

```
...
import net.sf.ehcache.CacheManager;
import net.sf.ehcache.constructs.web.PageInfo;
import net.sf.ehcache.constructs.web.filter.
PageFragmentCachingFilter;
...

public class CustomPageFragmentCachingFilter extends
PageFragmentCachingFilter {

...

//Override methods here
```

How it works...

Ehcache Fragment Caching is conveniently provided by the Ehcache web module. This module contains useful templates that are targeted at most common web fragment caching scenarios. You can further customize them to get more complex filtering behaviors to suit your needs.

We start by defining our typical Ehcache configuration and declaring the cache we desire for the fragment.

```
<cache name="FullPageCachingFilter"
        maxEntriesLocalHeap="1000"
        eternal="false"
        timeToIdleSeconds="300"
        timeToLiveSeconds="600">
```

Now, we define a subnode representing the persistence strategy we want for Ehcache to use. Simply said, this tells Ehcache that we are interested in using disk as another tier for storage. There are two persistent strategies that are useful for our purpose:

- none – no offload of cache entries to the disk; default mode
- localTempSwap – provides temporary local disk usage

> There are other persistent strategies available for Ehcache and Terracotta proprietary solutions. For further information visit http://ehcache.org/documentation/configuration/fast-restart#cache-persistence-implementation.

We select the `localTempSwap` option to swap cache entries between the disk and memory.

```
<persistence strategy="localTempSwap"/>
```

We then define the filter(s) and the filter mappings that we wish to apply in our project's `web.xml` file.

```
<!-- EhCache Full Page Cache Filter -->
  <filter>
    <filter-name>FullPageCachingFilter</filter-name>
    <filter-class>
            com.foo.filters.FullPageCachingFilter
        </filter-class>
  </filter>

  <filter-mapping>
    <filter-name>FullPageCachingFilter</filter-name>
```

```xml
        <url-pattern>/application/pageCache.action</url-pattern>
    </filter-mapping>
```

If you wish to just use the Ehcache default filters then do (refer to Ehcache web Java docs for other filters).

```xml
    <!-- EhCache Full Page Cache Filter -->
      <filter>
        <filter-name>SimplePageCachingFilter</filter-name>
        <filter-class>
                net.sf.ehcache.constructs.web.filter.
SimplePageCachingFilter
            </filter-class>
      </filter>
```

Then, we create a custom filter to add our own behaviors:

```java
    import net.sf.ehcache.constructs.web.filter.PageFragmentCachingFilter;
    ...

    public class CustomPageFragmentCachingFilter extends
    PageFragmentCachingFilter {
    ...
```

There's more...

In this recipe's source code sample you can find a basic Struts 2 web application using Ehcache as the fragment cache provider. It implements the recipe steps and provides insight in greater detail on how to manage configuration and filtering by showing how to build a custom filter. Please refer to *Appendix B, Setting Up the Source Code* (available for download at `http://www.packtpub.com/sites/default/files/downloads/0380OS_Appendix_B_Setting_Up_the_Source_Code.pdf`) for further information on how to build the recipe demo code.

Hibernate second-level caching (Intermediate)

In this recipe, we will cover the following topics:

- Ehcache as caching engine provider in a Hibernate project
- Hibernate second-level caching and its implementation

We will examine how to implement Hibernate second-level caching by integrating Ehcache as the cache provider. We also review what configuration is required to fully extend Ehcache in Hibernate.

Getting ready

Second-level caching is associated to the session factory object. This simply means that caching can be shared across multiple sessions instead of a per-session basis (first-level caching). Implementing second-level caching with Ehcache is one of the most utilized techniques in the industry.

In this recipe we discuss Ehcache integration with Hibernate version 3.x. If your requirement is to use Hibernate 4.x (and you are strictly using Terracotta's Big Memory Go), there are a few simple changes needed (replacing cache region factory classes with newly provided implementations). For further details visit `http://ehcache.org/documentation/integrations/hibernate`.

Refer to the `recipe5` project directory within the source code bundle for a fully working sample of this recipe content and further information related to this topic.

How to do it...

1. Add Ehcache and SLF4J library dependencies to your `POM.xml` file.

   ```xml
   <dependency>
       <groupId>net.sf.ehcache</groupId>
       <artifactId>ehcache-core</artifactId>
       <version>${ehcache.version}</version>
   </dependency>

   <dependency>
       <groupId>org.slf4j</groupId>
       <artifactId>slf4j-log4j12</artifactId>
       <version>${slf4j.version}</version>
   </dependency>
   ```

2. Create a blank XML file called `ehcache.xml` in the `resources` directory with the following content:

   ```xml
   <Ehcache xmlns:xsi="http://www.w3.org/2001/XMLSchema-instance"
   xsi:noNamespaceSchemaLocation="../../main/config/ehcache.xsd">

       ...

       <!-- Tracks the timestamps of the most recent updates to particular tables -->
       <cache name="org.hibernate.cache.UpdateTimestampsCache"
           maxEntriesLocalHeap="5000"
   ```

```xml
        eternal="true">
        <persistence strategy="localTempSwap"/>
    </cache>

    <!-- This cache is used if you use a query cache without
setting a name    -->
    <cache name="org.hibernate.cache.StandardQueryCache"
        maxEntriesLocalHeap="5"
        eternal="false"
        timeToLiveSeconds="120">
        <persistence strategy="localTempSwap"/>
    </cache>
```

3. Add the following entries to your `hibernate.cfg.xml` file:

```xml
...
<!-- use EhCache provider -->
<property name="cache.provider_class">
net.sf.ehcache.hibernate.EhCacheProvider
</property>

<!-- Enable Hibernate Second Level Cache (default = false) -->
<property name="hibernate.cache.use_second_level_cache">true</property>

<!-- Enable Hibernate Query Cache (default = false) -->
<property name="hibernate.cache.use_query_cache">true</property>
...
```

4. Add the following annotations to your Hibernate models:

```java
@Entity
@Table(name = "movies")
@Cacheable
@Cache(usage = CacheConcurrencyStrategy.READ_ONLY, region = "entityCache")
public class MovieEntity implements Serializable {
```

How it works...

Hibernate second-level caching is achieved relatively easily with Ehcache. We start by defining the cache configuration we want for a particular domain object. We also include two useful cache utilities that can alleviate some issues while invoking cache queries and tracking updates to cached tables.

```xml
<!-- Tracks the timestamps of the most recent updates to particular tables -->
<cache name="org.hibernate.cache.UpdateTimestampsCache"
       maxEntriesLocalHeap="5000"
       eternal="true">
    <persistence strategy="localTempSwap"/>
</cache>

<!-- This cache is used if you use a query cache without setting a name -->
<cache name="org.hibernate.cache.StandardQueryCache"
       maxEntriesLocalHeap="5"
       eternal="false"
       timeToLiveSeconds="120"
            memoryStoreEvictionPolicy="FIFO">
        <persistence strategy="localTempSwap"/>
</cache>
```

Note that we defined a subnode representing the persistence strategy we want for Ehcache to use. Simply said, this tells Ehcache that we are interested in using disk as another tier for storage. There are two persistent strategies that are useful for our purpose:

- `none` – no offload of cache entries to the disk; default mode
- `localTempSwap` – provides temporary local disk usage

> There are other persistent strategies available for Ehcache and Terracotta proprietary solutions. For further information visit `http://ehcache.org/documentation/configuration/fast-restart#cache-persistence-implementation`.

We select `localTempSwap` in order to be able to swap cache entries between the memory and disk.

We then edit the hibernate configuration file in order to let it know that we want to use second-level caching and Ehcache as the main provider:

```xml
<!-- use EhCache provider -->
<property name="cache.provider_class">
net.sf.ehcache.hibernate.EhCacheProvider
</property>

<!-- Enable Hibernate Second Level Cache (default = false) -->
<property name="hibernate.cache.use_second_level_cache">true</property>
```

Instant Effective Caching with Ehcache

```
<!-- Enable Hibernate Query Cache (default = false) -->
<property name="hibernate.cache.use_query_cache">true</property>
```

Finally, annotate our domain classes to include caching:

```
@Entity
@Table(name = "movies")
@Cacheable
@Cache(usage = CacheConcurrencyStrategy.READ_ONLY, region =
"entityCache")
public class MovieEntity implements Serializable {
```

In this case, the region is the name of the cache defined in `ehcache.xml`. The Usage attribute can have different values depending on your needs. For further information, please refer to the *Hibernate cache* documentation at `http://docs.jboss.org/hibernate/orm/3.3/reference/en/html/performance.html#performance-cache-mapping`.

There's more...

In this recipe's source code sample you can find a basic Hibernate application using Ehcache as the second-level cache provider. It implements the recipe steps and provides insight in greater detail on how to manage configuration and the code needed for successfully cache domain objects. Please refer to *Appendix B, Setting Up the Source Code* (available for download at `http://www.packtpub.com/sites/default/files/downloads/0380OS_Appendix_B_Setting_Up_the_Source_Code.pdf`) for further information on how to build the recipe demo code.

The Ehcache Search API (Advanced)

In this recipe, we will cover the following topics:

- The Ehcache Search API
- Implementing search queries and criteria conditions
- We will examine how to implement the Ehcache Search API. We also discuss how to improve performance of your caching solution as well as further information to make it scalable by adapting Ehcache to your applications OOP model.

Getting ready

The Ehcache Search API allows us to query and search for elements that are already cached. This is achieved thanks to the ability to use indexing on keys and/or values pertaining to the object being cached. Ehcache provides queries that let us create arbitrary complex searches based on conditions, making this tool indispensable for professional caching.

Refer to the recipe6 project directory within the source code bundle for a fully working sample of this recipe content and further information related to this topic.

How to do it...

1. Add Ehcache and SLF4J dependencies to your POM.xml file.

```
<dependency>
  <groupId>org.slf4j</groupId>
    <artifactId>slf4j-log4j12</artifactId>
  <version>1.7.2</version>
</dependency>
<dependency>
  <groupId>net.sf.ehcache</groupId>
    <artifactId>ehcache</artifactId>
    <version>2.6.0</version>
  <type>pom</type>
</dependency>
```

2. Add the searchable tag to your ehcache.xml file (to enable search) and search attributes to map your POJO getters:

```
<cache name="employeeCache" maxElementsInMemory="100" eternal="true" overflowToDisk="false">

    ...

    <!-- Adding EhCache searchable capabilities -->
    <searchable>

            <searchAttribute name="firstname" expression="value.getFirstName()"/>

            <!-- Adding a custom attribute extractor for performance reason -->
        <searchAttribute name="lastname"
                            class="com.foo.cache.LastNameAttributeExtractor"/>

            <searchAttribute name="profile" expression="value.getProfile()"/>

            <searchAttribute name="social" expression="value.
```

```xml
            getSocialNumber()"/>

        <!-- Profile Children Nodes -->
        <searchAttribute name="department"
                         expression="value.getProfile().
getDepartment()"/>

            <searchAttribute name="role"   expression="value.
getProfile().getRole()"/>

            <searchAttribute name="salary"
                             expression="value.getProfile().
getSalary()"/>

        </searchable>
</cache>
```

3. Create a map to hold references to the search attributes defined previously in step 2:

```
/**
 * load the attributes (as defined in ehcache.xml)
 * and store them in the reusable Cache Attributes Map
 **/
HashMap<String, Attribute<?>> cacheAttributes = new
HashMap<String, Attribute<?>>();

cacheAttributes.put("lastname", cache.getSearchAttribute("lastna
me"));
cacheAttributes.put("profile", cache.
getSearchAttribute("profile"));
cacheAttributes.put("department", cache.getSearchAttribute("depart
ment"));
cacheAttributes.put("role", cache.getSearchAttribute("role"));
cacheAttributes.put("salary", cache.getSearchAttribute("salary"));
cacheAttributes.put("social", cache.getSearchAttribute("social"));
```

4. Create an attribute extractor to improve performance. This step is optional.

```
...
import net.sf.ehcache.search.attribute.AttributeExtractor;
import net.sf.ehcache.search.attribute.
AttributeExtractorException;

public final class LastNameAttributeExtractor implements
AttributeExtractor {

  private static final long serialVersionUID = 1L;
```

```java
    public Object attributeFor(Element element) throws
AttributeExtractorException {

      return attributeFor(element);
    }

    public Object attributeFor(Element element, String
attributeName) {

      return ((YourPojo) element.getValue()).getLastName();
    }

  }
```

5. Implement a method that uses the Ehcache Search API.

    ```java
    public List<Employee> searchEngineers() {

      log.info("Searching all employees whose role is: " + Role.
    ENGINEER);

      List<Employee> employees = new ArrayList<Employee>();

      //create EhCache Search API Query
      Query query = cache.createQuery();

      //cast attribute from HashMap
      Attribute<Role> attribute = (Attribute<Role>) cacheAttributes.
    get("role");

      //add query criteria like: 'select {key, value} from Employee
    where role = ${@param role}'
      query.addCriteria(attribute.eq(Role.ENGINEER));

      //get the results list and loop on them
      Results results = query.execute();

      for(Result result : results.all()){
        /*
        log.info("Key: " + result.getKey());
        log.info("Value: " + result.getValue());
        log.info("Value Class: " + result.getValue().getClass());
        */
    ```

Instant Effective Caching with Ehcache

```
        Employee employee = (Employee) result.getValue();
        employees.add(employee);
    }

    return employees;
}
```

How it works...

Ehcache provides an easy-to-use Search API that allows us to retrieve objects from the cache layer based on conditions and other criteria. The implementation resembles one of the simple JDBC SQL queries.

The Ehcache Search API searches for data elements that are already cached. If your look in lookup searches for an entry that is not stored in cache, it will simply not return it (cache miss). In that case, you need to make sure to look it up in the data source and store it in cache so that it can later be searched and retrieved successfully.

We start by editing the Ehcache configuration by adding the searchable directive. This tells Ehcache that for that particular cache we want it to be searchable.

```
<cache name="employeeCache" maxElementsInMemory="100" eternal="true" overflowToDisk="false">

    <!-- Adding EhCache searchable capabilities →
    <searchable>...</searchable>

</cache>
```

We then define the search attributes. These are index mappings that tell Ehcache what attribute of your object you want to be searchable and a name to refer to it (always use `value` as your object reference).

```
    <!-- Adding EhCache searchable capabilities -->
    <searchable>
        ...
        <searchAttribute name="firstname" expression="value.getFirstName()"/>
        ...
    </searchable>
```

Now, in our code we need to create a map to hold attributes (not strictly necessary but a good practice and a convenient way to access the attributes in an ordered way).

```
HashMap<String, Attribute<?>> cacheAttributes = new HashMap<String, Attribute<?>>();
cacheAttributes.put("lastname", cache.getSearchAttribute("lastname"));
```

```
      cacheAttributes.put("profile", cache.getSearchAttribute("profile"));
      ...
```

Finally, we create methods (at your convenience) that hold the search queries' logic.

```
      public List<Employee> searchEngineers() {

        //create EhCache Search API Query
        Query query = cache.createQuery();

        //cast attribute from HashMap
        Attribute<Role> attribute = (Attribute<Role>) cacheAttributes.
      get("role");

        //add query criteria like: 'select {key, value} from Employee where
      role = {ROLE}
        query.addCriteria(attribute.eq(Role.ENGINEER));

        //get the results list and loop on them
        Results results = query.execute();

      ...
```

Optionally, if your cache object layer is complex, you will want to implement a custom accessor that can help you to increase performance while lookups. This can be easily achieved by implementing the Ehcache `AttributeExtractor` interface and redefining the behavior you desire. The procedure is just like if you were defining an index in a SQL table.

```
      ...
      import net.sf.ehcache.search.attribute.AttributeExtractor;
      import net.sf.ehcache.search.attribute.AttributeExtractorException;

      public final class LastNameAttributeExtractor implements
      AttributeExtractor {

      ...

        //using last name as the attribute extractor
        public Object attributeFor(Element element, String attributeName) {

          return ((YourPojo) element.getValue()).getSomeAttrName();
        }
```

For configuring the Ehcache Search API in distributed environments, visit Terracotta's *Ehcache Search API* documentation at http://ehcache.org/documentation/apis/search#ehcache-backed-by-the-terracotta-server-array.

There's more...

In this recipe's source code sample you can find a basic Java application using the Ehcache Search API. It implements the recipe steps and provides insight in greater detail on how to manage configuration and the code needed for successfully searching cached objects. Please refer to *Appendix B, Setting Up the Source Code* (available for download at http://www.packtpub.com/sites/default/files/downloads/0380OS_Appendix_B_Setting_Up_the_Source_Code.pdf) for further information on how to build the recipe demo code.

The custom eviction algorithm (Advanced)

In this recipe, we will cover the following topics:

- What an eviction algorithm is and how it works
- Creating custom eviction algorithms using Ehcache

We will examine how to implement a custom eviction algorithm for our cached objects. We will re-use the Ehcache library classes as the basis for our own eviction algorithm.

Getting ready

Eviction algorithms are used to determine when to evict (or simply eject) an element from the cache layer when a certain condition has been met (for example, its life duration).

Ehcache also provides built-in eviction algorithms that you can use. However, there may be scenarios where you will want to control how to eject cached objects, and may want your code to react upon specific conditions when this event dispatches.

> An example of such a scenario may be to implement an LIRS caching algorithm to prevent suboptimal performance on the cache layer weak access locality (a typical LRU problem). For further details refer to http://en.wikipedia.org/wiki/LIRS_caching_algorithm.

Currently, Ehcache defines the following default eviction algorithms:

- LRU – Least Recently Used; this is the default one
- LFU – Least Frequently Used
- FIFO – First In First Out

In the following sections, we show how to construct our own eviction algorithm implementation.

Instant Effective Caching with Ehcache

> Refer to the `recipe5` project directory within the source code bundle for a fully working sample of this recipe content and further information related to this topic.

How to do it...

1. Add Ehcache and SLF4J dependencies to your `POM.xml` file.

   ```xml
   <dependency>
     <groupId>net.sf.ehcache</groupId>
     <artifactId>ehcache</artifactId>
     <version>2.6.0</version>
      <type>pom</type>
   </dependency>
   <dependency>
     <groupId>org.slf4j</groupId>
     <artifactId>slf4j-log4j12</artifactId>
     <version>1.7.2</version>
   </dependency>
   ```

2. Add a cache to your configuration `ehcache.xml` (sample-only) file.

   ```xml
   <Ehcache xmlns:xsi="http://www.w3.org/2001/XMLSchema-instance"
   xsi:noNamespaceSchemaLocation="../../main/config/ehcache.xsd">

   <!-- store only 12 elements (see maxEntriesLocalHeap property) -->
     <cache   name="personCache"
              maxEntriesLocalHeap="12"
              eternal="false"
              overflowToDisk="false"
              timeToIdleSeconds="300"
              timeToLiveSeconds="600"
              statistics="true"/>

         ...
   ```

3. Create your new eviction policy by extending Ehcache's `AbstractPolicy` class:

   ```
       ...

       import net.sf.ehcache.Element;
       import net.sf.ehcache.store.AbstractPolicy;

       public class RndPolicy extends AbstractPolicy {

         //Our custom cache eviction policy (Random Replacement Cache)
   ```

```java
    public static final String NAME = "RND";

    @Override
    public String getName() {
      return NAME;
    }

    /**
     * Read the elements cache metadata and compares both with our
     * custom comparison algorithm. In this simple case, we are simply
     * using the creationTime metadata to determine element longevity.
     *
     * Comparing in Ehcache works as described below:
     * if returns true => second element is preferable for eviction
     * if returns false => first element is preferable for eviction
     */
    @Override
    public boolean compare(Element element1, Element element2) {

      /**
       * 50% chances of getting a false comparing
       */
      if(RNG.getValue() > 5){
          log.debug("--- random value generated in RND Policy: " + false);
          return false;

      } else {
          log.debug("--- random value generated in RND Policy: " + true);
          return true;
      }
    }

}
```

4. Tell Ehcache to use our new eviction policy.

   ```
   ...
   manager = new CacheManager(EHCACHE_CONFIG_LOCATION);
   cache = manager.getCache(CACHE_NAME);

   //set new eviction algorithm
   cache.setMemoryStoreEvictionPolicy(new RndPolicy());

   log.info("Eviction Policy set: " + cache.
   getMemoryStoreEvictionPolicy().getName());
   ...
   ```

5. Implement a cache event listener for seeing eviction in action. This step is optional.

   ```
   import net.sf.ehcache.event.CacheEventListener;

   public class CacheDelegateEventListener implements
   CacheEventListener {

     @Override
     public void notifyElementPut(Ehcache cache, Element element)
         throws CacheException {

       log.debug("Event Notification: :: Element Put ::" + element);
     }

     @Override
     public void notifyElementEvicted(Ehcache cache, Element element)
   {

       log.debug("Event Notification: :: Element Evicted ::" +
   element);
     }

     ...
   ```

How it works...

Supporting custom eviction algorithms is a relatively easy task in Ehcache. We start by defining a normal cache definition that we will like to use for our objects. Then, we create our custom policy by extending the `AbstractPolicy` class included in the Ehcache source library and overriding some of its methods.

```
import net.sf.ehcache.store.AbstractPolicy;

public class CustomPolicy extends AbstractPolicy {

  @Override
  public boolean compare(Element element1, Element element2) {

  ...
```

The `compare` method is the most important one, as this is used to determine which element is a candidate for eviction. Here we can implement almost any comparing algorithm we wish. Then, we need to tell Ehcache that we want it to use our new shiny algorithm. We do this by utilizing the `Cache` class' `setMemoryStoreEvictionPolicy` method:

```
cache.setMemoryStoreEvictionPolicy(new CustomPolicy());
```

If you want to implement a cache event listener, all you need to do is to implement Ehcache's `CacheEventListener` interface and react to the event in any way you want.

```
import net.sf.ehcache.event.CacheEventListener;

public class CacheDelegateEventListener implements CacheEventListener
{

  @Override
  public void notifyElementEvicted(Ehcache cache, Element element) {
      ...
}
```

The `notifyElementEvicted` function will not trigger as soon as the cached element is actually evicted. Its reference will remain until the cache memory gets cleaned up (assigned heap threshold has been reached). If you are evicting from disk, it will indeed trigger as soon as the element is evicted.

There's more...

In this recipe's source code sample you can find a basic Java application using the custom eviction algorithm (also known as a **policy**). It implements the recipe steps and provide insight in greater detail on how to manage the configuration and the code needed for successfully implementing an eviction policy from scratch. Please refer to *Appendix B, Setting Up the Source Code* (available for download at `http://www.packtpub.com/sites/default/files/downloads/0380OS_Appendix_B_Setting_Up_the_Source_Code.pdf`) for further information on how to build the recipe demo code. Consult the Ehcache documentation on how to configure caching eviction in distributed environments.

Out-of-process distributed caching (Intermediate)

In this recipe, we will cover the following topics:

- What out-of-process distributed caching is and why it is useful
- Setting up a RESTful cache server using Ehcache
- We will examine how to set up out-of-process distributed caching with the Ehcache cache server. This utility is provided by the Terracotta folks to ease the integration process with external systems via web services, such as SOAP and RESTful.

Getting ready

Out-of-process caching is a way of distributing your caching needs in a different JVM and/or infrastructure. Ehcache provides a convenient deployable WAR file that works on most web containers/standalone servers whose mission is to provide an easy API interface to distributed cache. At the moment of writing, you can download it from `http://sourceforge.net/projects/ehcache/files/ehcache-server/`, or you can include it in your Maven POM and will be delivered as a WAR file.

The cache server requires no special configuration on the Tomcat container. However, if you are running GlassFish, Jetty, WebLogic, or any other application server (or servlet container), there are minimal configuration changes to do. Please refer to the Ehcache cache server documentation for details on these.

While using the RESTful interface, it is important to note that you have three ways to set the MIME type for exchanging data back and forth to the cache server, namely Text/XML, application/JSON, and application/x-java-serialized-object.

Instant Effective Caching with Ehcache

You can use any programming language to invoke the web service interface and cache your objects (except for application/x-java-serialized-object for obvious reasons).

 Refer to the `recipe8` project directory within the source code bundle for a fully working sample of this recipe content and further information related to this topic.

How to do it...

1. Add Ehcache and Ehcache cache server dependencies to your `POM.xml` file.

   ```xml
   <dependency>
       <groupId>net.sf.ehcache</groupId>
       <artifactId>ehcache-server</artifactId>
       <version>1.0.0</version>
       <type>war</type>
   </dependency>

   <dependency>
     <groupId>net.sf.ehcache</groupId>
     <artifactId>ehcache</artifactId>
     <version>2.6.0</version>
     <type>pom</type>
   </dependency>
   ```

2. Edit `ehcache.xml` in the cache server to hold your cache setup (the cache name is very important).

   You can find this file here: `${CACHE_SERVER}/WEB-INF/classes/ehcache.xml`.

   ```xml
   <?xml version="1.0" encoding="UTF-8"?>
   <ehcache xmlns:xsi="http://www.w3.org/2001/XMLSchema-instance"
           xsi:noNamespaceSchemaLocation="ehcache.xsd"
           updateCheck="true" monitoring="autodetect"
           dynamicConfig="true">

     <!-- Set cache eternal (of course not to do in production) -->
     <cache name="remoteCache"
            maxElementsInMemory="10000"
            eternal="true"
            diskPersistent="true"
            overflowToDisk="true"/>

     ...
   ```

3. Disable the SOAP interface in the cache server `web.xml` (since we are going to use RESTful) file:

   You can find this file here: `${CACHE_SERVER}/WEB-INF/web.xml`.

```xml
<?xml version="1.0" encoding="UTF-8"?>
<web-app xmlns="http://java.sun.com/xml/ns/javaee"
         xmlns:xsi="http://www.w3.org/2001/XMLSchema-instance"
         xsi:schemaLocation="http://java.sun.com/xml/ns/javaee
         http://java.sun.com/xml/ns/javaee/web-app_2_5.xsd"
         version="2.5">

  ...

  <!--
SOAP Servlet
Comment out (or remove) to disable SOAP Web Services

<servlet>
    <servlet-name>EhcacheWebServiceEndpoint</servlet-name>
    <servlet-class>com.sun.xml.ws.transport.http.servlet.WSServlet</servlet-class>
    <load-on-startup>1</load-on-startup>
</servlet>
<servlet-mapping>
    <servlet-name>EhcacheWebServiceEndpoint</servlet-name>
    <url-pattern>/soap/EhcacheWebServiceEndpoint</url-pattern>
</servlet-mapping>
<session-config>
    <session-timeout>60</session-timeout>
</session-config>
<listener>
    <listener-class>
        com.sun.xml.ws.transport.http.servlet.WSServletContextListener
    </listener-class>
</listener>

-->

  ...
```

4. Make your objects-to-be-cached serializable:

   ```
   import java.io.Serializable;

   public final class Item implements Serializable {
   ```

5. Invoke the RESTful (or SOAP) interface to save/retrieve/delete cached objects:

   ```
   ...
   public void saveItemInCache(String key, Serializable item) {

     //sample URL: http://localhost:8080/ehcache/rest/cacheName/{id}
     //here cacheName is the cache name you set up in the cache-
   server ehcache.xml
     String url = CACHE_SERVER_URL + "cacheName" + "/" + key;

     //initialize Apache HTTP Client
     client = new DefaultHttpClient();

     //create Cache Element to be sent
     Element element = new Element(key, item);

     //serialize object to be sent to EhCache Server
     byte[] itemToByteArray = SerializationUtils.serialize(element);

     //create PUT request
     HttpPut putRequest = new HttpPut(url);

     //set header to read java-serialized-object mime type
     putRequest.setHeader("Content-Type", "application/x-java-
   serialized-object");

     ...
   ```

How it works...

The Ehcache cache server utility is a versatile tool that lets us distribute cache engines in a very flexible way. It provides a very simple API exposure via RESTful or SOAP-based web services.

We start by editing the `ehcache.xml` configuration file within the cache server application by adding a cache that we would like to use for our cached objects:

```
...

<!-- Set cache eternal (of course not to do in production) -->
<cache name="remoteCache"
```

```
            maxElementsInMemory="10000"
            eternal="true"
            diskPersistent="true"
            overflowToDisk="true"/>
    ...
```

 The cache name defined here is very important because this will be the endpoint of our RESTful URL pattern that the cache server will identify and use.

Then, we need to edit the web.xml file within the cache server application (located in {CACHE-SERVER}/WEB-INF/) in order to comment out (or completely remove) service definitions that we are not going to use (that is, SOAP if you are using RESTful or vice versa).

```
    <!--
SOAP Servlet
Comment out to disable SOAP Web Services

<servlet>
    <servlet-name>EhcacheWebServiceEndpoint</servlet-name>
    <servlet-class>com.sun.xml.ws.transport.http.servlet.WSServlet</servlet-class>
    <load-on-startup>1</load-on-startup>
</servlet>

    ...
```

In order to cache an object (specially a Java object), we need to make it serializable simply by implementing the Serializable interface (this is not a requirement for MIME types different from the application/x-java-serialized-object).

```
    import java.io.Serializable;

    public final class Item implements Serializable {
```

Finally, we invoke the RESTful endpoint from our code to store/retrieve/delete the object from/to the cache layer.

```
    //sample URL: http://localhost:8080/ehcache/rest/cacheName/{id}
    //here cacheName is the cache name you set up in the cache-server
    ehcache.xml
    String url = CACHE_SERVER_URL + "cacheName" + "/" + key;

    //set header to read json mime type
    putRequest.setHeader("Content-Type", "application/json");
```

It is important to note here that the `cacheName` URL parameter represents the cache name you defined in the ehcache.xml configuration file in the cache server application. You have defined your cache name as follows:

```
<!-- Set cache eternal (of course not to do in production) -->
<cache name="remoteCache"
       maxElementsInMemory="10000"
...
```

Now, your URL would be something like this:

```
//sample URL: http://localhost:8080/ehcache/rest/remoteCache/{id}
```

Here, `id` is just the key value you assign to the cached object.

Finally, you just use any http/SOAP client library (or Java default Net API classes) to invoke the web service. In the case of RESTful services, you need to be aware that the HTTP method sent determines whether you are storing, updating, retrieving, or deleting a cached item. They are as follows:

- `GET /{cache}/{element}`: This retrieves an object by its key from the O-O-P cache layer.
- `PUT /{cache}/{element}`: This stores an item in the O-O-P cache layer.
- `DELETE /{cache}/{element}`: This deletes an item from the O-O-P cache layer.
- `HEAD /{cache}/{element}`: This retrieves metadata (cache configuration values) from the O-O-P cache layer.
- `OPTIONS /{cache}/{element}`: This returns the WADL describing operations.

If you are deploying an Ehcache cache server (standalone or clustered) application, you should change the default context name as well as enable security (disabled by default).

For changing the context you can edit the file `${CACHE_SERVER}/META-INF/context.xml` and place your desired context name.

As for security, look for the file `${CACHE_SERVER}/WEB-INF/server_security_config.xml_rename_to_activate` and open it to read the instructions.

There's more...

In this recipe's source code sample you can find a basic Java application using the Ehcache out-of-process caching solution—cache server. It implements the recipe steps and provides insight in greater detail on how to manage configuration and the code needed for successfully implementing a cache server client from scratch. Please refer to *Appendix B, Setting Up the Source Code* (available for download at `http://www.packtpub.com/sites/default/files/downloads/0380OS_Appendix_B_Setting_Up_the_Source_Code.pdf`) for further information on how to build the recipe demo code.

Ehcache monitoring and logging (Intermediate)

In this recipe, we will cover the following topics:

- Monitoring an Ehcache-enabled web application
- Configuring logging correctly with standard libraries
- Integrating Ehcache with third-party monitoring solutions

We will examine how to monitor and log an Ehcache-based application. We will use third-party open source Java Melody for viewing Ehcache activities as well as other important factors. We will also look at how to configure SLF4J (Ehcache logging interface) with Log4j, as this is the standard Java logging library used in many projects worldwide.

Getting ready

Caching is all about memory fluctuations, disk writing/reading, and performance statistics; so it rapidly becomes a production issue if it is not correctly set up. One way to determine a successful caching implementation is, not surprisingly, monitoring and logging.

In this recipe we delve into the details of integrating an open source production quality monitoring tool called Java Melody (`https://code.google.com/p/javamelody/`). This tool comes with a web interface out of the box that presents a simple yet powerful monitor. Also, we show how to set up logging libraries (SLF4J and Log4j) to communicate properly.

 Refer to the `recipe9` project directory within the source code bundle for a fully working sample of this recipe content and further information related to this topic.

How to do it...

1. Add Ehcache, Log4j, SLF4J, and Java Melody dependencies to your `POM.xml` file.

   ```
   <dependency>
     <groupId>net.sf.ehcache</groupId>
     <artifactId>ehcache</artifactId>
     <version>2.6.0</version>
   </dependency>
   <dependency>c
     <groupId>org.slf4j</groupId>
     <artifactId>slf4j-log4j12</artifactId>
     <version>1.6.4</version>
   </dependency>
   ```

Instant Effective Caching with Ehcache

```xml
<dependency>
  <groupId>log4j</groupId>
  <artifactId>log4j</artifactId>
  <version>1.2.16</version>
</dependency>

<dependency>
  <groupId>net.bull.javamelody</groupId>
  <artifactId>javamelody-core</artifactId>
  <version>1.32.1</version>
</dependency>
```

2. Edit your cache configuration XML file to include some cache.

```xml
<Ehcache xmlns:xsi="http://www.w3.org/2001/XMLSchema-instance"
xsi:noNamespaceSchemaLocation="../../main/config/ehcache.xsd">

...

<cache name="employeeCache"
            maxElementsInMemory="50"
            eternal="false"
            overflowToDisk="false"
            statistics="true"
            memoryStoreEvictionPolicy="FIFO" />

...
```

3. Create and configure a context parameter/filter definition in your `web.xml` file to set up Java Melody monitoring configuration (both Spring and non-Spring configurations are shown).

```xml
<web-app xmlns="http://java.sun.com/xml/ns/javaee"
xmlns:xsi="http://www.w3.org/2001/XMLSchema-instance"
xsi:schemaLocation="http://java.sun.com/xml/ns/javaee
version="2.5">
...
 <!-- IF USING SPRING -->
 <context-param>
      <param-name>contextConfigLocation</param-name>
      <param-value>
            classpath:net/bull/javamelody/monitoring-spring.xml
            /WEB-INF/applicationContext.xml
      </param-value>
</context-param>
```

...

```xml
    <!-- IF NOT USING SPRING -->
    <filter>
            <filter-name>monitoring</filter-name>
            <filter-class>net.bull.javamelody.MonitoringFilter</filter-class>
    </filter>
    <filter-mapping>
            <filter-name>monitoring</filter-name>
            <url-pattern>/*</url-pattern>
    </filter-mapping>
    <listener>
            <listener-class>net.bull.javamelody.SessionListener</listener-class>
    </listener>
```

   ...

4. Implement caching using any of the variants we have seen in the previous recipes:

   ```java
   @Repository("employeeDao")
   public class EmployeeDaoImpl extends JdbcDaoSupport implements EmployeeDao {

   ...

       @Cacheable("employeeCache")
       public List<Employee> findAll() {
           String sql = "SELECT * FROM employees";
           return getJdbcTemplate().query(sql,
                           new BeanPropertyRowMapper<Employee>(Employee.class));
       }

   ...

   }
   ```

5. Access your localhost URL with your web application context and `?monitoring` to access the Java Melody web monitoring tool.

   ```
   http://localhost:8080/yourAppContext?monitoring
   ```

6. Tail your terminal output to see the Ehcache default output (the Tomcat output is shown).

   ```
   tail -f {TOMCAT_HOME}/logs/catalina.out
   ```

How it works...

We start by adding the dependencies we will need for logging SLF4J and Log4j, monitoring Java Melody, and Ehcache. By adding the `slf4j-log4j12.jar` bridge, we ensure that the Ehcache built-in logging library (`slf4j`) can talk to `log4j`. This way we don't have to configure anything else to ensure proper Ehcache logging in our console output.

Once that is done, we create our typical `ehcache.xml` file with some cache configuration we would like to apply.

```xml
<Ehcache xmlns:xsi="http://www.w3.org/2001/XMLSchema-instance"
xsi:noNamespaceSchemaLocation="../../main/config/ehcache.xsd">
...
    <cache name="employeeCache" maxElementsInMemory="50" ...
```

We then edit the `web.xml` file (in a web application) to include either a `filter` (for non-spring applications) or a `context-param` (for spring applications) that contains information about Java Melody configuration.

```xml
<!-- IF NOT USING SPRING -->
<filter>
      <filter-name>monitoring</filter-name>
      <filter-class>net.bull.javamelody.MonitoringFilter</filter-class>
</filter>

...

<!-- IF USING SPRING -->
<context-param>
     <param-name>contextConfigLocation</param-name>
     <param-value>
          classpath:net/bull/javamelody/monitoring-spring.xml
          /WEB-INF/applicationContext.xml
     </param-value>
</context-param>
```

Instant Effective Caching with Ehcache

Assuming that we have implemented caching on some of your Java objects using the techniques shown in the previous recipes, we start our server and point to the following URL:

```
http://localhost:8080/yourAppContext?monitoring
```

Generate some activity and you will see the following (at the bottom of the web page):

📁 **Data caches**

1 cache(s) on Daniels-MacBook-Pro.local@10.0.1.9   ⊟ Details

Cache	% used of memory cache	Number of objects in memory	Number of objects on disk	% of efficiency of memory cache (memory hits/hits)	% of efficiency of cache (hits/accesses)	Configuration
employeeCache	2	1	0	100	83	ehcache [maxElementsInMemory = 50, overflowToDisk = false, eternal = false, timeToLiveSeconds = 0, timeToIdleSeconds = 0, memoryStoreEvictionPolicy = FIFO, diskPersistent = false]

🗑 Clear caches   Configuration reference

Last collect time: 328 ms
Display time: 36 ms
Memory overhead estimate: < 1 Mb

JavaMelody 1.32.1

> Terracotta offers a monitoring add-on tool called **Ehcache Monitor** that is not open source and commercially licensed (free for development use). You can, however, test the 30 days trial and decide if it is the tool you need. For further information visit `http://ehcache.org/downloads/monitor`.

There's more...

In this recipe's source code sample you can find a basic web application using Spring and Apache Wicket running on an embedded Jetty server. It has Java Melody enabled for tracking cache as well as the other goods that it provides. Please refer to *Appendix B, Setting Up the Source Code* (available for download at `http://www.packtpub.com/sites/default/files/downloads/0380OS_Appendix_B_Setting_Up_the_Source_Code.pdf`) for further information on how to build the recipe demo code.

Ehcache transactional support (Advanced)

In this recipe, we will cover the following topics:

- Ehcache atomic caching operations and its benefits
- Configuring Ehcache for supporting transactions

We will examine how atomic transactional operations are configured in Ehcache. We first get a firm grasp on transactional modes and code requirements within the transaction context. Then, we will go over the details on implementing a local transactional cache in cluster mode using **Terracotta Server Array** (for details refer to the *Ehcache and Terracotta Server Array (Advanced)* recipe).

Getting ready

Transactions guarantee that all operations are to be completed successfully or fully discarded if an error occurs. In our context an error means some sort of exception (for example, an error in the datasource). If this happens within a transaction, all suboperations are rolled back and the original state is recovered.

Ehcache offers us a robust API to provide transactionality to our cache layer. There are four modes available:

- XA_Strict
- XA
- Local
- Off

The default mode is Off. XA (extended architecture) transactions refer to global transactions that may span multiple resources (a transaction manager or multiple data sources). Local transactions in contrast allow us to define cache operations to be atomic in the same `CacheManager` instance (the single-phase commit), giving us independency of external transaction managers.

At a code level, our objects need to be serializable (implement the `Serializable` interface) and we must override the `equals()` and `hashCode()` object methods in order to be eligible for transactional caching.

In this recipe we show you how to set up Ehcache local transactional caching. Please see the more info section for further relevant information on XA transactions.

If you are unsure of which mode to use, Terracotta recommends using the following tips:

- **Local**: Atomic transactions that are the result of cached calculations and operations.
- **XA**: Atomic transactions on multiple data stores (sacrificing data sync in case of a crash).

Instant Effective Caching with Ehcache

▶ **XA_Strict**: Atomic transactions on multiple data stores (guaranteed disaster recovery sacrificing performance).

 Refer to the `recipe10` project directory within the source code bundle for a fully working sample of this recipe content and further information related to this topic.

How to do it...

1. Add Ehcache and SLF4J dependencies to your `POM.xml` file.

   ```xml
   <dependency>
       <groupId>org.slf4j</groupId>
       <artifactId>slf4j-log4j12</artifactId>
       <version>1.7.2</version>
       <scope>compile</scope>
   </dependency>
   <dependency>
     <groupId>net.sf.ehcache</groupId>
     <artifactId>ehcache</artifactId>
     <version>2.6.0</version>
     <type>pom</type>
   </dependency>
   ```

2. Edit your Ehcache configuration XML file to add the following content:

   ```xml
   <Ehcache xmlns:xsi="http://www.w3.org/2001/XMLSchema-instance"
   xsi:noNamespaceSchemaLocation="../../main/config/ehcache.xsd">

   ...

    <cache   name="someCache"
             maxElementsInMemory="100"
             ...
             transactionalMode="local">

     <terracotta consistency="strong"/>

    </cache>
   ```

3. Edit your domain objects to be serializable and override the `hashCode()` and `equals()` methods.

```java
public class MyDomainObject implements Serializable {

...
   private int id;
  private String myDomainObjectProperty1;
  private String myDomainObjectProperty2;
  private double myDomainObjectProperty3;
  ...

    @Override
    public boolean equals(Object obj) {
        //our class is supposed to be inmutable
          if (obj == null || obj.getClass() != getClass()) {
            return false;
        }

        //you should implement your own object comparing function
        MyDomainObject alt = (MyDomainObject) obj;

        return id == alt.id
            && (myDomainObjectProperty1 == guest.myDomainObjectProperty1
                || (myDomainObjectProperty1 != null &&
                 myDomainObjectProperty1.equals(guest.getMyDomainObjectProperty1())))
            && (myDomainObjectProperty2 == guest.myDomainObjectProperty2
                || (myDomainObjectProperty2 != null &&
                myDomainObjectProperty2 .equals(guest.getMyDomainObjectProperty2())));
    }

    @Override
    public int hashCode() {
        return id.hashCode() + (int) myDomainObjectProperty3;
    }

    ...

}
```

4. Initialize the `CacheManager` and `Ehcache` references in your code.

   ```
   import net.sf.ehcache.CacheManager;
   import net.sf.ehcache.Ehcache;

   ...

   CacheManager cacheManager = new CacheManager();
   Ehcache someCache = cacheManager.getCache("someCache");

   ...
   ```

5. Get the transaction controller from the Ehcache transactional API.

   ```
   import net.sf.ehcache.TransactionController;
   ...
   TransactionController txController = cacheManager.
   getTransactionController();
   ...
   ```

6. Decorate your methods (beginning and end) with the transaction directives.

   ```
   ...
   transactionController.begin();

   //do some caching based operations here
   externalService.calculateSomethingWithCache();

   transactionController.commit();
   ...
   ```

How it works...

Local mode transactions in Ehcache are easy to set up, as we have complete independence of external transaction managers and/or server configuration. This mode is useful when you do operations over cached elements and want a transactional process to occur among them. It is also worth mentioning that this mode is supported in clustered mode too.

We start by adding transactional support to the Ehcache configuration. This simply means that we need to specify the transactional mode we want for our cache.

```
<cache name="someCache"
       maxElementsInMemory="100"
       ...
       transactionalMode="local">
```

Instant Effective Caching with Ehcache

If our application is clustered in Terracotta Server Array, we need to specify this in the Ehcache configuration file. Please note that we must set the consistency parameter to `"strong"`, as follows:

```
<terracotta consistency="strong"/>
```

Then, we define all our cached objects classes `Serializable` and we override a couple of methods, `hashCode()` and `equals()`, inherited from the Java `Object` root class (required).

```
public class MyDomainObject implements Serializable {

    @Override
    public boolean equals(Object obj) {...}

    @Override
    public int hashCode() {...}
```

Now, we need to initialize our cache manager and cache as we normally do (note that `cache` is an Ehcache instance).

```
...
CacheManager cacheManager = new CacheManager();
Ehcache someCache = cacheManager.getCache("someCache");
```

Then, we create an instance that refers to the transaction controller (available from the Ehcache API). This controller wraps all the transactional directives over the cache layer.

```
...
TransactionController txController = cacheManager.
getTransactionController();
```

It's time for the good stuff. Select the method(s) in your code that you want to provide transactional processing to. Decorate those methods with the following try-catch code:

```
try {
        //initiate transaction
        transactionController.begin();

        //do some caching based operations here
        externalService.calculateSomethingWithCache();

        //submit transaction
        transactionController.commit();

    } catch (Exception ex) {

        //if something goes wrong, roll everything back
        transactionController.rollback();

    }
```

That will provide a transactional operation and we'll be able to keep data integrity for critical parts of our cache-based system. Note that since this is operating atomically, there is a performance penalty. Therefore, you should analyze where transactions would fit properly. Naturally, you can mix transactional caches with regular caches in your `ehcache.xml` file and hence use them where appropriate.

Last but not least, you can catch exceptions that can get generated over the transaction progress, namely `TransactionException`, `TransactionInterruptedException`, and `TransactionTimeoutException`.

The exception cause is self-explanatory for the ones mentioned previously. It is worth mentioning that whenever a transaction begins, changes are not visible to other threads until they are committed. This pretty much matches with the transactional behavior of databases or any other datasource.

> Ehcache offers strong support for XA transactions with JTA synchronization. These depend on transaction managers usually provided by the application server where your app lives (WebLogic, JNDI, Bitronix, and so on). You can specify which one to use. For more information on these, refer to the Ehcache documentation at `http://ehcache.org/documentation/apis/transactions`.

There's more...

In this recipe's source code sample you can find a basic Java application that implements transactional caching and simulates all conditions that could happen in production environments. This demo shows how to configure caching and how to decorate your transactional methods to handle cache atomically. Please refer to *Appendix B, Setting Up the Source Code* (available for download at `http://www.packtpub.com/sites/default/files/downloads/0380OS_Appendix_B_Setting_Up_the_Source_Code.pdf`) for further information on how to build the recipe demo code.

Ehcache and Terracotta Server Array (Advanced)

In this recipe, we will cover the following topics:

- What Terracotta Server Array is and its clustered environment
- Integrating Ehcache and Terracotta Server Array
- Using the Terracotta TSA-DSO Monitor tool

We will examine how to distribute Ehcache in a clustered environment using Terracotta Server Array. This Terracotta product offers built-in Ehcache for easier integration and configuration. We can combine the in-process cache (that one living in our application) with the benefits of a clustered cache backup. This process is known as **DSO** (**Distributed Shared Objects**).

Getting ready

Terracotta Server Array (**TSA**) is an in-memory data platform providing faster and consistent access to data. It comes as a clustered array of nodes from a basic two-node tandem to a multinode array (completely configurable). It is open source and freely available here (at the moment of writing): `http://terracotta.org/downloads/open-source/catalog`.

Refer to the `recipe11` project directory within the source code bundle for a fully working sample of this recipe content and further information related to this topic.

As of Terracotta's March 4, 2013 release of BigMemory 4.0, Terracotta will no longer issue updates to the open-source Terracotta Server Array. Terracotta recommends the free production version of BigMemory Max, which offers all the functionality of the open-source Terracotta Server Array and much more. To explore and download the free version of BigMemory Max, visit `http://terracotta.org/products/bigmemorymax`.

How to do it...

1. Add Ehcache, SLF4J, and Terracotta toolkit dependencies to your `POM.xml` file.

```
<dependency>
  <groupId>org.terracotta</groupId>
  <artifactId>terracotta-toolkit-1.6-runtime</artifactId>
  <version>5.4.0</version>
</dependency>

<dependency>
  <groupId>net.sf.ehcache</groupId>
  <artifactId>ehcache</artifactId>
  <version>2.6.0</version>
  <type>pom</type>
</dependency>

<dependency>
    <groupId>org.slf4j</groupId>
    <artifactId>slf4j-log4j12</artifactId>
    <version>1.7.2</version>
    <scope>compile</scope>
```

        </dependency>

2. Create a blank XML file named `tc-config.xml` in your project root directory with the following content:

   ```
   <?xml version="1.0" encoding="UTF-8"?>

   <tc:tc-config xmlns:tc="http://www.terracotta.org/config"
                 xmlns:xsi="http://www.w3.org/2001/XMLSchema-instance"
                 xsi:schemaLocation="http://www.terracotta.org/schema/terracotta-4.xsd">

     <servers>
       <server host="127.0.0.1" name="localhost" bind="0.0.0.0">
         <dso-port>9510</dso-port>
         <jmx-port>9520</jmx-port>
         <data>target/terracotta/server/data</data>
         <logs>target/terracotta/server/logs</logs>
         <statistics>target/terracotta/server/statistics</statistics>
       </server>
       <update-check>
         <enabled>true</enabled>
       </update-check>
     </servers>

     <system>
           <configuration-model>development</configuration-model>
     </system>

     <clients>
       <logs>target/terracotta/clients/logs/%(tc.nodeName)</logs>
     </clients>

     <application>
        <dso>

              <instrumented-classes>
                  <include>
                      <class-expression>
                           your.domain.cached.object.here
                      </class-expression>
                  </include>
              </instrumented-classes>
              <roots>
   ```

Instant Effective Caching with Ehcache

```
                <root>
                    <field-name>
                        your.cache.manager.instance.here
                    </field-name>
                </root>
            </roots>
        </dso>
    </application>

</tc:tc-config>
```

3. Edit the `ehcache.xml` configuration file to enable TSA.

```
...

<cache name="applicationCache" maxElementsInMemory="500"
                               eternal="false"
                               overflowToDisk="false"
                               timeToIdleSeconds="3600"
                               timeToLiveSeconds="1800"
                               memoryStoreEvictionPolicy="LFU">

    <!-- TERRACOTTA default scheme -->
    <terracotta/>

</cache>

<!-- Terracotta configuration -->
<terracottaConfig url="127.0.0.1:9510" />

...
```

How it works...

Enabling cluster-distributed caching in an Ehcache-based application is a seamless process if using Terracotta Server Array. This product comes integrated with Ehcache and other goods that make it a convenient choice for scaling distributed cache.

We start by including the Terracotta toolkit runtime, which is very important for our application to work properly. You may need to find out what toolkit version is suitable for your TSA version.

```
<dependency>
    <groupId>org.terracotta</groupId>
    <artifactId>terracotta-toolkit-1.6-runtime</artifactId>
    <version>5.4.0</version>
</dependency>
```

Then, we would like to override the TSA configuration for our application purposes. We do this by setting our own `tc-config.xml` (the Terracotta configuration) file to configure our application-cached objects (the ones we wish to cache in the cluster).

```xml
...
<application>
  <dso>
    <!-- Here you can instrument n cached objects -->
      <instrumented-classes>
        <include>
          <class-expression>
            your.domain.cached.object.here
          </class-expression>
        </include>
      </instrumented-classes>
    <!-- Here you define who manages caching in your app -->
      <roots>
        <root>
          <field-name>
            your.cache.manager.instance.here
          </field-name>
        </root>
      </roots>
  </dso>
</application>
...
```

Finally, we need to let Ehcache know that we want to use distributed clustered cache using TSA. We do this by setting the following parameters in `ehcache.xml` (can be done programmatically too):

```xml
<cache name="someCache" ... >

  <!-- Enable TERRACOTTA default scheme -->
  <terracotta/>

</cache>

<!-- Terracotta configuration (point to your IP:PORT if running in a server) -->
  <terracottaConfig url="127.0.0.1:9510" />
```

And that's about it. Our application will run normally, but it will remotely cluster our cached objects so that we have high availability caching layer. You can configure TSA to suit your project needs. So for instance, you can specify the number of cluster nodes, what replication technique to use, what topology to follow, and so on.

Instant Effective Caching with Ehcache

If you would like to monitor your cluster and your cache, Terracotta Server Array includes a very useful tool called dev-console (`${TERRACOTTA_HOME}/bin/`), where you can measure everything related to your cluster.

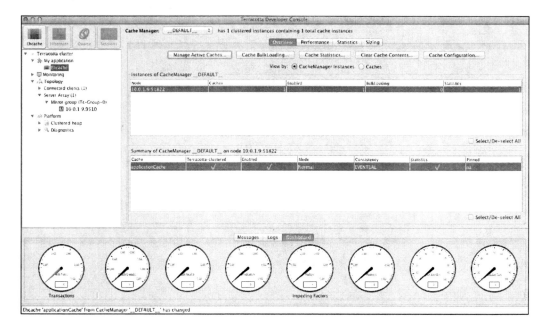

 Terracotta offers proprietary distributed in-memory caching called BigMemory Go and BigMemoryMax. Out of the two, BigMemory Go is free for development purposes and comes with 32 GB. These products are the Terracotta's replacements for TSA. For more information, visit `http://www.terracotta.org/downloads`.

There's more...

In this recipe's source code sample you can find a basic Java application that distributes its cache layer in a Terracotta Server Array cluster. This demo shows how to configure caching and communicate with the cluster from your own code. Please refer to *Appendix B, Setting Up the Source Code* (available for download at `http://www.packtpub.com/sites/default/files/downloads/03800S_Appendix_B_Setting_Up_the_Source_Code.pdf`) for further information on how to build the recipe demo code.

Datasource read overloading (Intermediate)

In this recipe, we will cover the following topics:

- What the thundering herd problem is
- Avoiding read overloading with multithreaded blocking cache

We will examine how to implement a technique known as blocking cache to avoid the typical thundering herd problem. We will base our efforts by re-using Ehcache's already-provided constructs. We will also demonstrate how to use them with a simple program (included in the source code bundle for this book).

Getting ready

Datasource read overloading (also known as **thundering herd**) happens when a cached element is requested simultaneously and that element is no longer available in the cache (a cache miss), perhaps because it was evicted, or it was cleared due to some business logic, and so on.

Whatever the reason is, all concurrent threads will try to repopulate the cache element by first querying the datasource (be it a database, message queue, file, and so on). This is when the thundering herd problem is evident; you will see all those threads asking the datasource directly for that element instead of only one thread asking for it, caching it, and the rest of the threads can synchronize again from the cache layer (and not query the datasource).

How to solve this problem?

What comes to mind seems simple to implement. You just need to have one and only one thread querying the datasource when a cache miss happens and have the rest to read the cache layer again.

Indeed there are several ways to solve it. Some are easy but nonperformant, others are hard to implement. Lock striping tends to be the most common solution for hash key based subsets. Nevertheless, Ehcache already provides useful constructs that you can use, so you do not have to worry about this problem. The constructs are available in the `net.sf.ehcache.constructs` package.

In this recipe we will use the `BlockingCache` class (a blocking decorator for Ehcache) that allows concurrent reads in the cache. If the element is null, other threads will block until an element with the same key is back in the cache.

Refer to the `recipe12` project directory within the source code bundle for a fully working sample of this recipe content and further information related to this topic.

How to do it...

1. Add Ehcache and SLF4J dependencies to your POM.xml file.

   ```xml
   <dependency>
     <groupId>net.sf.ehcache</groupId>
     <artifactId>ehcache</artifactId>
     <version>2.6.5</version>
     <type>pom</type>
   </dependency>

   <dependency>
       <groupId>org.slf4j</groupId>
       <artifactId>slf4j-log4j12</artifactId>
       <version>1.7.2</version>
       <scope>compile</scope>
   </dependency>
   ```

2. Create a blank XML file called ehcache.xml in the resources directory with the following content:

   ```xml
   <?xml version="1.0" encoding="UTF-8"?>
   <ehcache xmlns:xsi="http://www.w3.org/2001/XMLSchema-instance"
            xsi:noNamespaceSchemaLocation="ehcache.xsd"
            updateCheck="false"
            monitoring="off"
            dynamicConfig="true">

       <cache name="applicationCache" maxElementsInMemory="500"
                                      eternal="true"
                                      overflowToDisk="false"
                                      memoryStoreEvictionPolicy="LFU"/>

   </ehcache>
   ```

3. Update your cache manager programmatically to include the blocking cache decorator:

   ```java
   ...

   import net.sf.ehcache.CacheManager;
   import net.sf.ehcache.Ehcache;
   import net.sf.ehcache.Element;
   import net.sf.ehcache.constructs.blocking.BlockingCache;

   public final class CacheDelegate {
   ```

```java
    private static final String EHCACHE_CONFIG_FILE = "ehcache.xml";
    private static final String CACHE_NAME = "applicationCache";

    private CacheManager manager;
    private BlockingCache blockingCache;
    private Ehcache cache;

    public CacheDelegate() {

      manager = new CacheManager(
          this.getClass().getClassLoader().
    getResourceAsStream(EHCACHE_CONFIG_FILE));

            cache = manager.getEhcache(CACHE_NAME);

      blockingCache = new BlockingCache(cache);

      //replace default cache with decorated cache (Blocking Cache)
      manager.replaceCacheWithDecoratedCache(cache, blockingCache);
    }


    /**
    * Saves a message in cache layer. Currently just one value.
    * @param message a Message object (Custom)
    */
    public void saveMessageInCache(Message message) {

      log.debug("--- Adding element to cache layer ---");
      blockingCache.put(new Element(message.getId(), message));
    }

    ...
}
```

How it works...

While working on highly concurrent environments, problems with data access start to appear and cache is not an exception. To remediate this problem, Ehcache offers us a built-in solution that we can safely re-use and expect it to handle the majority of situations we might encounter in production environments.

We start by adding out a typical cache configuration that will dictate how we want to cache objects (ehcache.xml).

```
...
<cache name="applicationCache" maxElementsInMemory="500"
                eternal="false"
                overflowToDisk="false"
                memoryStoreEvictionPolicy="LFU"/>
...
```

The important piece of implementing the blocking cache is made programmatically. The reason for this is that it allows us a better thread handling and we can customize our code to match our business logic.

```
//cache needs to be an instance of Ehcache class
Ehcache cache = manager.getEhcache(CACHE_NAME);


//we create our BlockingCache instance here
BlockingCache blockingCache = new BlockingCache(cache);

//replace default cache with decorated cache (Blocking Cache)
  manager.replaceCacheWithDecoratedCache(cache,
blockingCache);
```

And that's all there is to it. You just use the `blockingCache` instance to interact with the cache layer (retrieve objects, put objects, and so on) as if you were using a `cache` instance (like we have done in previous recipes). This way you will easily avoid concurrency problems.

Ehcache offers another built-in decorator, `SelfPopulatingCache`, that automates the cache entry creation on demand. It not only extends `BlockingCache` (inherits all the functionality we have seen), but also allows cache clients (threads) not to worry if the cache entry is null. It manages null cache entries' self population behind the scenes. For further information, visit http://ehcache.org/apidocs/net/sf/ehcache/constructs/blocking/SelfPopulatingCache.html.

There's more...

In this recipe's source code sample you can find a basic Java application that simulates a high concurrent environment where thundering herd is expected to occur. This demo shows how to configure caching and how to decorate the cache manager with a cache decorator implementation. Please refer to *Appendix B, Setting Up the Source Code* (available for download at http://www.packtpub.com/sites/default/files/downloads/03800S_Appendix_B_Setting_Up_the_Source_Code.pdf) for further information on how to build the recipe demo code.

A
Core Concepts

This appendix exposes the cache basics every developer should be familiar with. This is solely intended to provide a synthesized theoretical background.

> Cache is a component that transparently stores data so that future requests for that data can be served faster.
>
> —Source: Wikipedia

Cache is a simple concept really; you may be applying it and probably don't realize it. For example, every time you query a database result for the customer's name and store that value in the session object, you are applying caching techniques. Simply put, your application does not need to query the database every single time that it needs that same value. Instead, it just retrieves it from the session object (in-memory), which as you might know is persistent.

Ehcache (`http://www.ehcache.org`) is a widely used, open source Java-based caching library that you can easily integrate with your Java projects. From a coder's perspective, Ehcache is just like using a Java Map instance that you need to configure in order to save results from external (or even internal) resources and data providers, so that you don't need to consult them too often in order to speed up your application. Terracotta provides an excellent Ehcache reference documentation on its website: `http://ehcache.org/documentation/get-started/` that all readers should be acquainted with. In this section, I will point out the most important topics that are necessary for a newcomer to understand the technology.

You may be wondering why you need Ehcache in your project anyways. Well, the truth is that you need to assess your project architecture and performance bottlenecks in order to decide whether Ehcache is suitable. If your project is being impacted by high data loads, high memory/CPU consumption, proven delays while serving content, latency in your web services layer, or even if you verify that your cluster is not performing adequately, it would be worth adding Ehcache to your project.

Core Concepts

The antagonism here is what to cache. Most developers are tempted with the idea that caching is useful for static data (data that remains constant during the application's life span). To help you answer this, think about what percentage of your application data is static. Usually, no more than 5 percent of your code is. Now, imagine if you could cache dynamic and/or transactional data (the sort of data that usually changes every few minutes). For that short time span, you are able to reduce some complex queries to the database, hence improving performance. Imagine the effect of this approach when hundreds of concurrent users are hitting this feature. You will start to see the dividends of implementing caching by speeding up your application as well as relaxing load in the datasource.

At a lower level, caching benefits are often dependent of the type of binding your application has. There are two types: CPU and I/O.

- **CPU bindings**: This refers to the processing computation that a certain algorithm requires, for example, when a piece of software generates and renders an image (often referred to as Image Processing). This is purely processing power, since there are algorithms (for example Fourier transforms) that are needed to be executed in order to generate the said image.
- **I/O bindings**: This refers to the process of read-write data. Usually, this type of binding is restricted to two realms: network and disk, for example, when a piece of software queries a database. This is a typical I/O operation that many production systems rely on.

In real-world projects you usually have a combination of both bindings into your application (at different levels). The key for a successful caching implementation is to identify which modules or results of your architecture need to be cached. How do you determine if caching will benefit your architecture? Short answer, there is no rule of thumb. However, in my opinion, there are three factors that can help you decide this:

- Reusability of cached components
- Data accessibility (read/write)
- Proportion of response time (cached versus noncached)

Determining caching efficiency is a delicate balance of these three factors. If you re-use a cached component (let's say some result of the database) but the response time is close to what you achieve without using caching, the benefits are not immediately evident. There are other factors as well that can help you predict somehow the benefit of integrating a caching solution into your application. I must stress, however, that even though this is important to know, Ehcache provides a fantastic tool to show cached elements statistics so that we can quantify rather than estimate, allowing us to tweak it at runtime and see the different results.

Appendix A

Cache usage patterns

Once you have determined that your project needs Ehcache, your next move should be to determine what usage pattern you will need to apply. Ehcache supports the following patterns:

- cache-aside
- cache-as-sor
- read-through
- write-through
- write-behind

cache-aside

This pattern is the most common approach. In simple words you consult the cache entity first and if it contains the requested data, it is retrieved (from now on we will refer to this behavior as a cache lookup). Otherwise, the application code queries the datasource directly. A disadvantage with this approach is its invasive nature; you may need to alter your data access layer in order to place logic to consult caching.

cache-as-sor

This pattern is all about using cache as your primary datasource. In this case, we are clearly separating concerns, which may sound attractive to OOP purists. And, it indeed has the advantage of not being code intrusive, leading to maintainability and scalability. However, for someone external to our development team it would not be as easy to decipher, since the implementation is completely hidden.

read-through

This pattern is similar to cache-aside while reading data, the difference being that you need to explicitly tell the cache engine how to read data when a cache lookup fails. For doing this, it is common to apply the factory design pattern (you could choose any that suits your needs though) and change the factory class signature by implementing a specific interface.

write-through

This pattern is similar to cache-aside while writing data, the difference being that the data writing to the system-of-record happens in the same thread.

Core Concepts

write-behind

The write-behind pattern let's you modify the writing time to the system-of-record. In simple words, it allows the caching system to write data at a later time (specified in the configuration) hence, not doing it in the same thread of execution. This is particularly useful because it writes data to the datasource outside the scope of the actual transaction.

There's more...

There are certain aspects that you also might need to take into account in order to successfully understand caching efficiency. I will start by the very root of it: caching processes. There are two types: in-process caching and out-process caching. These processes govern both single server and clustered applications, and are a very important decision on architecture.

In-process caching

In-process caching occurs when the caching layer is embedded directly in the application. This is the most common scenario. One simple example can be when you simply adjust your project to include the Ehcache layer. You handle all the cache policies within your application, and you code and modify behaviors of your application to include caching. Please refer to the following diagram:

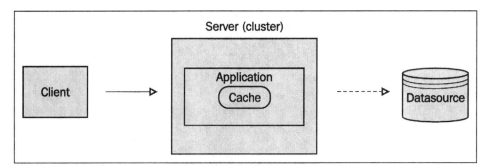

The following are the advantages of in-process caching:

- Simple implementation and maintenance
- Quick access to cached objects

The following are the disadvantages of in-process caching:

- Higher consumption of memory and/or CPU
- Increase in the garbage collector load
- Data inconsistency (multiple copies of objects stored at a large volume)

Appendix A

You may be wondering why I mentioned higher consumption of memory and CPU as one of the disadvantages. Isn't Ehcache supposed to benefit us on that? Well the truth is that caching has a cost for your server. How much? It all depends on how your application is bound to the underlying resources (CPU or I/O, refer to the precedent section). You should be clear that the real purpose of in-process caching is to actually *speed up* your application's performance primarily by *reducing* the load on the dependent parts of your architecture (for example, the database), hence providing *faster* access to objects. A load test analysis can help you determine whether it is worth adding in-process caching support. If it is not, you have another option: out-process caching.

Out-process caching

Out-process caching (often referred to as **Distributed Caching**) simply refers to having an externalized caching solution (often referred to as the cache server). In this case, your application talks directly to an externalized component (cache server) and gets data as if the cache server is the primary datasource. The communication happens through common means such as RMI and web services where the object is serialized and deserialized back and forth. Refer to the following figure:

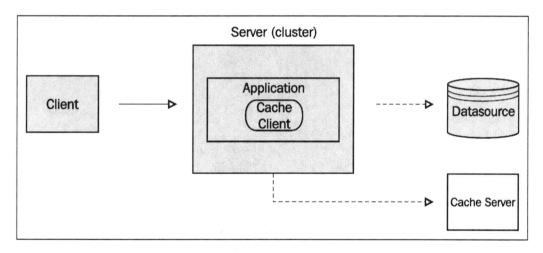

In this case you have another JVM instance in a different server. However, we must stress that for this architecture, you need to take into account networking constraints. How high is the network's latency? How fast the bit rate is? These and some other questions you will need to solve in order to determine whether it is worth adding this caching process. As a side note, the majority of the enterprise applications use this caching model. Usually, the caching architecture happens in the form of a distributed cache cluster that acts accordingly.

Core Concepts

The advantages of out-process caching are as follows:

- Decrease in the garbage collector load
- Effective memory and CPU memory increases
- Single shared object storage

The disadvantages of out-process caching are as follows:

- Requires network access
- Implementation is difficult

For more information on clustering visit `http://ehcache.org/documentation/user-guide/cache-topologies#distributed-caching-distributed-ehcache`.

> JCache (JSR-107) is an early draft of the Java Specification for Cache. While this is still in progress, it's expected to be completed in early 2013. This API specification will be implemented by the majority of active vendors: Terracotta (Ehcache), Oracle (Coherence), JBoss (Infinispan), IBM (eXtreme Scale), Google App Engine Java, SpringSource (GemFire), and others. Greg Luke, the founder of Ehcache, is an active member of this amazing project.

Thank you for buying
Instant Effective Caching with Ehcache

About Packt Publishing

Packt, pronounced 'packed', published its first book "*Mastering phpMyAdmin for Effective MySQL Management*" in April 2004 and subsequently continued to specialize in publishing highly focused books on specific technologies and solutions.

Our books and publications share the experiences of your fellow IT professionals in adapting and customizing today's systems, applications, and frameworks. Our solution based books give you the knowledge and power to customize the software and technologies you're using to get the job done. Packt books are more specific and less general than the IT books you have seen in the past. Our unique business model allows us to bring you more focused information, giving you more of what you need to know, and less of what you don't.

Packt is a modern, yet unique publishing company, which focuses on producing quality, cutting-edge books for communities of developers, administrators, and newbies alike. For more information, please visit our website: www.packtpub.com.

Writing for Packt

We welcome all inquiries from people who are interested in authoring. Book proposals should be sent to author@packtpub.com. If your book idea is still at an early stage and you would like to discuss it first before writing a formal book proposal, contact us; one of our commissioning editors will get in touch with you.

We're not just looking for published authors; if you have strong technical skills but no writing experience, our experienced editors can help you develop a writing career, or simply get some additional reward for your expertise.

Spring Roo 1.1 Cookbook

ISBN: 978-1-84951-458-3   Paperback: 460 pages

Over 60 recipes to help you speed up the development of your Java web applications using the Spring Roo development tool

1. Learn what goes on behind the scenes when using Spring Roo and how to migrate your existing Spring applications to use Spring Roo

2. Incrementally develop a Flight Booking enterprise application from scratch as various features of Spring Roo are introduced

3. Develop custom add-ons to extend Spring Roo features

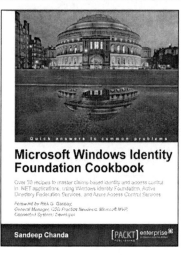

Microsoft Windows Identity Foundation Cookbook

ISBN: 978-1-84968-620-4   Paperback: 294 pages

Over 30 recipes to master claims-based identity and access control in .NET applications, using Windows Identity Foundation, Active Directory Federation Services, and Azure Access Control Services

1. Gain a firm understanding of Microsoft's Identity and Access Control paradigm with real-world scenarios and hands-on solutions

2. Apply your existing .NET skills to build claims-enabled applications

3. Includes step-by-step recipes on easy-to-implement examples and practical advice on real-world scenarios

Please check **www.PacktPub.com** for information on our titles

Infinispan Data Grid Platform

ISBN: 978-1-84951-822-2   Paperback: 150 pages

Making use of data grids for performance and scalability in Enterprise Java, using Infinispan from JBoss

1. Configure and develop applications using the Infinispan data grid platform
2. Follow a simple ticket booking example to easily learn the features of Infinispan in practice
3. Draw on the experience of Manik Surtani, the leader, architect, and founder of this popular open source project

Oracle Coherence 3.5

ISBN: 978-1-84719-612-5   Paperback: 408 pages

Create Internet-scale applications using Oracle's high-performance data grid

1. Build scalable websites and Enterprise applications using a market-leading data grid product
2. Design and implement your domain objects to work most effectively with Coherence and apply Domain Driven Designs (DDD) to Coherence applications
3. Leverage Coherence events and continuous queries to provide real-time updates to client applications

Please check www.PacktPub.com for information on our titles

CPSIA information can be obtained at www.ICGtesting.com
Printed in the USA
BVOW06s2032201213

339740BV00002B/56/P